Hard Press

A DISSERTATION SUBMITTED TO THE FACULTY OF THE GRADUATE SCHOOL OF ARTS AND LITERATURE IN CANDIDACY FOR THE DEGREE OF DOCTOR OF PHILOSOPHY (DEPARTMENT OF ENGLISH).

BY

OSCAR LUDVIG OLSON

ContentsIt was at the suggestion of Professor John M. Manly that I took up the study which has resulted in the following dissertation, and from him I have received much encouragement and valuable assistance on numerous occasions. I have profited by suggestions received from Professor Tom Peete Cross and Professor James R. Hulbert; and Professor Chester N. Gould has been unstinting in his kindness in permitting me to draw on his knowledge of the Old Norse language and literature. In addition to the aid received from these gentlemen, professors in the University of Chicago, I have received bibliographical information and helpful suggestions from Professor Frederick Klaeber, of the University of Minnesota; I have been aided in various ways by Professor George T. Flom, of the University of Illinois, particularly in preparing the manuscript for the press; and from others I have had assistance in reading proof. To all these gentlemen I am very grateful, and I take this opportunity to extend to them my sincere thanks.

INTRODUCTORY.

The following pages are the result of an investigation that has grown out of a study of *Beowulf.* The investigation has been prosecuted mainly with a view to ascertaining as definitely as possible the relationship between the Anglo-Saxon poem and the *Hrlfs Saga Kraka*, and has involved special consideration of two portions of the saga, namely, the *B[o.]varsttr*, and the *Frattr*, and such portions of the early literature in England and the Scandinavian countries as seem to bear some relationship to the stories contained in these two portions of the saga. Some of the results achieved may seem to be outside the limits of the main theme. But they are not without value in this connection, for they throw light on the manner in which the *Hrlfssaga* and some of the other compositions in question came to assume the form in which we now find them. Thus these results assist us in determining the extent to which the saga and the *Bjarkarmur* are related to *Beowulf.*

As the field under consideration has been the object of investigation by a number of scholars, much that otherwise would need to be explained to prepare the way for what is to be presented lies ready at hand, and this is used as a foundation on which to build further.

In order to give the reader who is interested in the subject, but has not made a special study of it, an idea of the problems involved, and the solutions that have been offered, the discussion is preceded by a brief summary of the principal conclusions reached by various scholars.

BIBLIOGRAPHY AND ABBREVIATIONS

Aarb.—Aarbger for nordisk Oldkyndighed og Historie, 1894.

Ark.—Arkiv fr Nordisk Filologi.

Ang.—Anglia.

Ant. Tid.—Antiquarisk Tidsskrift.

Beow.—Beowulf. The line numbering used is that of A.J. Wyatt's edition.

Beow., Child—*Beowulf and the Finnesburh Fragment*, translated by C.G. Child, 1904.

Beow. Stud.—Beowulf-Studien, by Gregor Sarrazin, 1888.

Beow. Unt.—Beowulf, Untersuchungen, by Bernhard ten Brink, 1888.

Beow. Unt. Ang.—Beowulf, Untersuchungen ber das angelschsische Epos und die lteste Geschichte der germanischen Seevlker, by Karl Mllenhoff, 1889.

Camb. Hist. Lit.—The Cambridge History of English Literature.

Chron.—Chronicles of England, Scotland, and Ireland, by Raphael Holinshed, edition of 1808.

Helt.—Danmarks Heltedigtning, by Axel Otrik, vol. I, 1903; vol. II, 1910.

Dan. Nor. Rig.—Danske og norske Riger paa de britiske er i Danevldens Tidsalder, by Johannes C.H. Steenstrup, 1882.

Eng. Nov.—The Development of the English Novel, by Wilbur L. Cross, 1914.

Dictionary of National Biography.

Eng. Stud.—Englische Studien.

Ext. Ch. Rol.—Extraits de la Chanson de Roland, by Gaston Paris, 1912.

Gest. Dan.—Gesta Danorum, by Saxo Grammaticus, edited by A. Holder, 1886.

Elton's Saxo—The First Nine Books of the Danish History of Saxo Grammaticus, translated by Oliver Elton, 1894.

Gesch. Alteng. Lit.—Geschichte der altenglischen Litteratur, by Alois Brandl (Paul's *Grundriss der germanischen Philologie*, 1908).

Heimsk.—Heimskringla, eller Norges Kongesagaer, by Snorre Sturlasson, edited by C.R. Unger, 1868.

Hist. Reg. Wald.—Historia Regis Waldei, by Johannes Bramis, edited by R. Imelmann, 1912.

Hist. Mer.—Historia Meriadoci, edited by J.D. Bruce, 1913.

Hrs. Bjark.—Hrlfs Saga Kraka og Bjarkarmur, edited by Finnur Jnsson. 1904.

Icel. Leg.—Icelandic Legends, collected by Jn Arnason, translated by George E. Powell and Eirkur Magnsson, 1864.

Mort. d'Arth.—Morte d'Arthur, by Sir Thomas Malory, Globe edition, 1871.

Norroen Fornkvi, edited by Sophus Bugge, 1867.

Nor. Tales—Norse Fairy Tales, selected and adapted from the translations of Sir George Webbe Dasent, 1910.

Folk. Huld. Even.—Norske Folke-og Huldre-Eventyr i Udvalg, by P. Chr. Asbjrnsen, revised edition by Moltke Moe, 1910.

Event. Sagn—Norske Folkeeventyr og Sagn, by O.T. Olsen, 1912.

Nor. Hist.—Det norske Folks Historie, by P.A. Munch, 1852.

Sagn—Norske Sagn, Christiania, 1902.

Notes, Beow.—Notes on Beowulf, by Thomas Arnold, 1898.

Oldn. Lit. Hist.—Den oldnorske og oldislandske Litteraturs Historie, by Finnur Jnsson.

Grundr.—Paul's *Grundriss der germanischen Philologie.*

P.B.B.—Paul and Braune's *Beitrge zur Geschichte der deutschen Litteratur.*

Pop. Tales—Popular Tales from the North, by George Webbe Dasent, 1859.

P.M.L.A.—Publications of the Modern Language Association of America.

Grettis.—The Saga of Grettir the Strong, Everyman's Library.

Sc. Folkl.—Scandinavian Folk-lore, by William A. Craigie, 1896.

Sc. Rer. Dan.—Scriptores Rerum Danicarum, edited by Jakob Langebek, 1772.

Macb.—Shakespeare's *Tragedy of Macbeth*, edited by William J. Rolfe, 1905.

Skjs.—Skj[o.]ldungasaga (*Aarbger for nordisk Oldkyndighed og Historie*, 1894).

Sn. Ed.—Snorri Sturluson, Edda, edited by Finnur Jnsson, 1900.

St. germ. Sag.—Studien zur germanischen Sagengeschichte; I *Beowulf*, by Friedrich Panzer, 1910.

St. Sag. Eng—Studien zur Sagengeschichte Englands; I Teil, *Die Wikingersagen*, by Max Deutschbein, 1906.

V[o.]lsungasaga (Fornaldarsogur Norrlanda, edited by Valdimar Asmundarson, vol. I, 1891).

Widsith (*The Oldest English Epic—Beowulf, Widsith, etc.*—translated by Francis B. Gummere, 1909).

Yel. Fair. Bk.—The Yellow Fairy Book, by Andrew Lang.

CONTENTS.

THE RELATION OF THE HRLFS SAGA KRAKA AND THE BJARKARMUR TO BEOWULF.

I

B[O.]VARSTTR.

The question whether Saxo Grammaticus' account of Biarco's fight with a bear or the account in the *Hrlfssaga* of Bjarki's fight with a winged monster is the earlier version of the story has been the subject of much discussion, as has also the possible identity of Bjarki's (Biarco's) exploit with one or both of Beowulf's exploits (his slaying of Grendel and the dragon). The latter problem is still further complicated by the introduction of two beasts in the *Bjarkarmur* where Saxo and the *Hrlfssaga* have only one, and the introduction in *Beowulf* of Grendel's mother, who makes her appearance in order to defend her offspring and also is slain.

In this dissertation an attempt will not be made to clear up the whole of this complicated matter. But an attempt will be made to solve some of the problems involved. It will be shown that the stories in the *Bjarkarmur* of the slaying of the wolf and the bear at the court of Hrolf Kraki[1] are based on the story in the *Hrlfssaga* of the slaying of the winged[2] monster. The explanation of the origin of the dragon and the interpretation of the whole dragon story in the *Hrlfssaga*, both of which have hitherto been wanting, will be given. From this it will be seen that this story in the *Hrlfssaga* is based on the story, related in the second book of Saxo's *Gesta Danorum*[3], of Bjarki's slaying the bear.

Earlier Opinions in Regard to the B[O.]VARSTTR, *the* BJARKARMUR, *and Related Matters.*

Gisli Brynjulfsson, the first writer, apparently, to call attention to the similarity between Beowulf's combat with Grendel and Bjarki's combat with the winged monster, identified the story in the *Hrlfssaga* of Bjarki's fight with the winged monster with the story in *Beowulf* of Beowulf's fight with Grendel. That it was a sea-monster (havjtte) that caused the trouble in Denmark, while it was a mountain-troll that caused the trouble in Norway, he thought was as characteristic as anything could be.[4]

Gregor Sarrazin would identify Bjarki with Beowulf. He calls attention to striking similarities between the stories about the two men and attempts to identify the word "B[o.]var," etymologically, with the word "Beowulf." The translator, as he calls the author of *Beowulf*, may, through misconception, have regarded "var," the second part of the name "B[o.]var," as "vargr" and translated it faithfully into AS. "wulf." This, combined with other changes, which he discusses and illustrates, that might have taken place in the name in its passage from very early Danish to Anglo-Saxon, could have caused the Scandinavian name "B[o.]var" to be rendered "B[=e]owulf" in Anglo-Saxon.[5]

Sophus Bugge thought that saga-characteristics earlier ascribed to Beowulf had been transferred, in Danish tradition, to Bjarki. The story of Bjarki's fight with the winged monster he regarded as acquired from contact with the story of Beowulf's fight with the dragon. He showed that the words "B[o.]var" and "B[=e]owulf" are not etymologically related, but that "B[o.]var" is the genitive of "b[o.]," meaning "battle," so that "B[o.]var Bjarki" means "Battle Bjarki." He called attention to the fact that Saxo regarded Bothvar's real name as Bjarki (Lat. Biarco), that the *Bjarkaml* was called after that name, and, furthermore, that Saxo ascribed to Bjarki the words "belligeri cepi cognomen".[6]

Sarrazin regards the story of Bjarki's journey from Sweden to Denmark and subsequent exploit there, with which he identifies the corresponding journey and exploit of Beowulf, as an embodiment of the Balder and Frey cult. He thinks it may be interpreted as the southward journey of the sun in the autumn and its contest with frost and mists when it reaches its southern limit (i.e., Denmark, according to the ancient conception of the people of the Scandinavian peninsula); or it may be interpreted as the introduction of the Balder-cult from Sweden into Denmark.[7]

Bernhard ten Brink agreed with Karl Mllenhoff,[8] that, on the one hand, there is really no similarity between the Beowulf story and Saxo's account of Bjarki, in which the blood-drinking episode is the main point, and, on the other, between Saxo's account and that in the *Hrlfssaga*, which has too much the nature of a fairy tale to be ancient tradition. He agreed with Bugge, that Bjarik's combat with the winged monster shows contact with the story of Beowulf's fight with the dragon.[9]

Sarrazin, replying to ten Brink, scouts the idea that a poem, such as *Beowulf*, which was completely unknown in England after the eleventh century, should, after this time, be well known in Scandinavian countries and exert a notable influence there.[10]

G. Binz does not think that Sarrazin's attempt to identify Bjarki with Beowulf is sufficiently substantiated and shows by a list of names,[11] dating from the twelfth century and found in the Northumbrian *Liber Vitae*, that the story about Bjarki was probably known at an early date in northern England.[12]

Sarrazin thinks that perhaps Beowulf married Freawaru, Hrothgar's daughter, as, similarly, Bjarki, according to the *Hrlfssaga*, married Drifa, the daughter of Hrothgar's nephew, Hrolf Kraki; that the troll which supports Hrolf Kraki's enemies in Hrolf's last battle is a reminiscence of the dragon in *Beowulf*; and that, owing to the change of taste and other causes that occurred in the course of time, the Beowulf story developed into the form in which it is found in the Bjarki story in the *Hrlfssaga*.[13]

Thomas Arnold concedes that there may be a faint connection between the Bjarki story and the Beowulf story, but he rejects Sarrazin's theory that the Anglo-Saxon poem is a translation from the Scandinavian (see p. 8).[14]

B. Symons takes the story of Bjarki's fight with the winged monster to be a fusion of the story of Beowulf's fight with Grendel and that of his fight with the dragon.[15]

R.C. Boer identifies Bjarki with Beaw. In the West-Saxon line of kings, Beaw succeeded Scyld; in the poem *Beowulf*, Beowulf, the Danish king, succeeded Scyld; in Saxo's account, Frothi I succeeded Scyld. Frothi is represented as having killed a dragon.

According to the *Hrlfssaga*, Bjarki killed a dragon. As Beaw in one account occupies the same position in the royal line as Frothi in another and Beowulf, the Dane, in a third, Boer thinks that Bjarki's exploit and Frothi's exploit are the same one and that to Beowulf, the Dane, the same exploit was also once attributed. In Saxo's account, Bjarki is a king's retainer; and Boer thinks his exploit has been differentiated from that of Frothi, who is a king. In *Beowulf*, he thinks, the exploit has been transferred from Beowulf, the Danish king, to Beowulf, the Geat, and that the differentiation of the deed into two exploits has been retained—Beowulf, as a king's retainer, slaying Grendel, and later, as a king, killing a dragon. This identifies Bjarki's slaying of the winged monster with Beowulf's slaying of Grendel. In Saxo's account of Bjarki, Boer thinks that the dragon has been stripped of its wings and changed to a bear.[16]

Finnur Jnsson regards the story in the *Hrlfssaga* of Bjarki's slaying the winged monster as a reflection, though a feeble one, of the Grendel story in *Beowulf*.[17]

Axel Olrik, who, more extensively than any other writer, has entered into the whole matter, of which the problems here under consideration form a part, does not think there is any connection between *Beowulf* and the *Hrlfssaga*.[18] He regards the stories in the *Bjarkarmur* of Bjarki's slaying the wolf and Hjalti's slaying the bear as earlier compositions than the corresponding story in the *Hrlfssaga*.[19] The addition of "Bothvar" to Bjarki's name he thinks was acquired among the Scandinavians in the north of England,[20] where the Bjarki story, by contact with the story of Siward, Earl of Northumberland, acquired the further addition of Bjarki's reputed bear-ancestry.[21] The stories in the *Grettissaga*, *Flateyjarbk*, and *Egilssaga* to which counterparts are found in *Beowulf*, he believes to have been acquired by contact either with the Beowulf legend or, perhaps, with the Anglo-Saxon epic itself.[22]

Finnur Jnsson thinks that the stories in the *Bjarkarmur* of Bjarki's slaying the wolf and Hjalti's slaying the bear are later compositions than the story in the *Hrlfssaga* of Bjarki's slaying the winged monster, and supports this opinion by maintaining that the monster in the saga is a reminiscence, though altered and faded, of Grendel in *Beowulf*.[23]

Sarrazin regards the cowardly, useless Hott, Bjarki's companion, as a personification of the sword Hrunting, which fails Beowulf in his fight with Grendel's mother. But Hjalti, as Hott is called after he has become brave and strong, he regards as a personification of the giant-sword with which Beowulf dispatches Grendel's mother. Sarrazin would also identify the giant-sword, which is said to have a golden hilt (gylden hilt), with the sword Gullinhjalti in the *Hrlfssaga*.[24]

Max Deutschbein sees a connection between the Bjarki story and the *Gesta Herwardi* that would tend to establish the story in the *Bjarkarmur* as earlier than the corresponding story in the *Hrlfssaga*.[25]

H. Munro Chadwick, basing his opinion on the similarity between the career of Bjarki and that of Beowulf, thinks there is good reason for believing that Beowulf was the same person as Bothvar Bjarki.[26]

Alois Brandl does not think that Beowulf and Bjarki were the same person. He calls attention to the difficulty involved in the fact, which, he says, Olrik has emphasized, that "Bjarki" is etymologically unrelated to "Bir"; and of troll fights, he says, there are many in Scandinavian literature.[27]

William Witherle Lawrence thinks that "we may have to do with late influence of *Beowulf* upon the *Hrlfssaga*".[28] He identifies "gylden hilt" with Gullinhjalti.[29] He regards the stories in the *Bjarkarmur* of Bjarki's slaying the wolf and Hjalti's slaying the bear as earlier compositions than the story in the *Hrlfssaga* of Bjarki's slaying the winged monster,[30] which, in agreement with Olrik, he regards as "a special late elaboration peculiar to the *Hrlfssaga*." He regards Saxo's story as earlier than the stories in the *Bjarkarmur*.[31] He refers to Mogk as believing that the Bjarki story in the saga is a werewolf myth into which the Grendel motive is woven.[32] He quotes a passage from Heusler, in which Heusler states that he regards the story in the *Bjarkarmur* of the fight with the bear as earlier than the story in the saga of the fight with the winged monster and that, furthermore, Beowulf's fight with Grendel has been transferred to Bjarki.[33] Lawrence also calls attention to the fact that Gering thinks there is unmistakable similarity between the Grendel story and the story of Bjarki's fight with the winged monster.[34]

Friedrich Panzer identifies Bjarki with Beowulf and regards the story in question in the *Hrlfssaga* as a later composition than the corresponding stories in the *Bjarkarmur*, which he identifies with the Grendel story.[35] "Gylden hilt" he identifies with Gullinhjalti;[36] and Hott-Hjalti, whom Sarrazin regards as a personification of swords in *Beowulf*, he identifies with Hondscio, Beowulf's companion who is devoured by Grendel.[37]

The Story in the HRLFSSAGA *of Bjarki's Slaying the Winged Monster.*

It appears to the writer that the key to the explanation of much that has been the subject of dispute, or has remained unexplained, in the story about Bothvar Bjarki in the *Hrlfssaga* is the influence of the fictitious (in part, also historical) life of Siward, Earl of Northumberland under Canute the Great and succeeding kings.

The life of Siward, briefly summarized from the *Dictionary of National Biography*,[38] is as follows.

Siward, Earl of Northumberland, called Digera, or the strong, a Dane, is said to have been the son of a Danish jarl named Birn. According to legend he was descended from a white bear and a lady, *etc.*[39] As a matter of fact, he probably came to England with Canute and received the earldom of Deira after the death of Eadwulf Cutel, the Earl of Northumbria, when the Northumbrian earldom appears to have been divided. He married lfld, daughter of Ealdred, Earl of Bernicia, the nephew of Eadwulf Cutel. In 1041 he was employed by Hardecanute, along with Earls Godwin and Leofric, to ravage Worcestershire. Later he became Earl of Northumberland and probably also of Huntingdon.

He upheld Edward the Confessor in his quarrels with Godwin in 1051. In pursuance of the king's command, Siward invaded Scotland both by sea and land with a large force in 1054. The King of Scotland was Macbeth, who had slain his predecessor, Duncan I, the husband of a sister or cousin of the earl, and Siward's invasion was evidently undertaken on behalf of Duncan's son Malcolm. A fierce battle took place on July 27th; the Scots were routed, Macbeth fled, and Malcolm appears to have been established as King of Cumbria in the district south of the Firths of Forth and Clyde. Siward died at York in 1055. Siward and his son Osbeorn, called by Shakespeare "Young Siward," appear in *Macbeth*.

The legendary life of Siward is found in two Latin versions in Langebek's *Scriptores Rerum Danicarum*, vol. III. These two versions Olrik designates as A (anonymous; p. 288) and B (Bromton; p. 300).[40] According to B, an earl of royal descent in the kingdom of the Danes had an only daughter, who went with her maidens for a walk in a neighboring wood. They met a bear, whereupon the maidens fled and the daughter was seized by the bear and carried off. In the course of time she gave birth to a son, whose name was Bern and who bore marks, in the shape of a bear's ears, of his paternity. Bern had a son, whose name was Siward. According to A, Siward is removed by three generations more from his bear-ancestor, the line of descent being Ursus (the bear), Spratlingus, Ulsius (should be Ulfius), Beorn (with the cognomen Beresun), Siward.

According to A, where the account is a little more detailed than in B, Siward, who was given the cognomen Diere (large), was a brave and powerful man, who, disdaining the succession to his father's earldom in Denmark, set sail with one vessel and fifty chosen companions, and arrived at the Orkney Islands. On one of the islands was a dragon that had done much damage by killing men and cattle. To show his strength and bravery, Siward entered into a combat with the dragon and drove it from the island. Thence he set sail for Northumberland, and there, he heard, there was another dragon. During the search for this dragon, he met an old man sitting on a hill. He inquired of the man as to the whereabouts of the dragon. But the man, calling him by name, told him that he sought the dragon in vain, and directed him to continue his journey and proceed till he came to a river called Thames, on whose bank was situated a city by the name of London. "And there," he said, "you will find the king of that region, who will enlist you in his service and in a short time bestow land upon you." As a token of the trustworthiness of his prediction, the old man drew from the folds of his garment a banner, called Ravenlandeye, and presented it to Siward.

Siward accepted the banner and proceeded to London, where he was summoned by King Edward to meet him at Westminster. Siward obeyed the summons and was enlisted in the service of the king, who promised him the first position of honor to become vacant in the kingdom. On this visit to the king, he slew Tosti in order to avenge an imagined insult and demanded and received Tosti's earldom of Huntingdon, which had thus become vacant. Some time after he also received the earldoms of Northumberland, Cumberland, and Westmoreland.

Later the Norwegians made war on the king; but Siward defeated them and avenged many fold the insults and injuries sustained by the king, thus fulfilling the prophecy "that Divine Providence would permit to be born from the union of a rational with an irrational creature, *i.e.*, from the union of a woman with a bear, a man who would wreak vengeance on the enemies of the illustrious and glorious King of England."

In the course of time, Dunewal, King of the Scots, was ejected from his kingdom. He sought the aid of Siward, who gathered an army and proceeded as far as Dundee, when news was brought him that his subjects in Northumberland had risen in insurrection and slain his son Osbertum (Osbernum) Bulax. Compelled to return he was roused to such anger that he sank his sword into a rock leaving a mark that could be seen, the author says, in his day. Siward restored to the king the territory seized by the rebels, and returned home and inflicted severe punishment on his enemies.

B has some variations from the account in A, but none of these variations are of present significance.

The transformation of Siward from an historical character, in regard to whom we have authentic information, into the hero of a saga the first part of which is of the "fornaldarsaga" type, the latter part of the "Islndingasaga" type,[41] is quite remarkable. He must have made a deep impression on the minds of his contemporaries and remained a hero in oral tradition long after the historical events of his life had been forgotten.

Olrik, who has done work of great importance in this field, offers a discussion of the legendary life of Siward in the *Arkiv fr nordisk Filologi*, vol. XIX, from which it seems desirable to quote some passages for the light they throw on the development of this saga in England.

"Tagen som helhed er Sivards saga den mrkelige forening af ventyrlig og historisk sagastil."

* * * * *

"I dragekampene og i Odinskikkelsen, er der nr tilslutning til norrn tradition; her m de i Nordengland bosatte Nordmnd have gjort sig gldende med et berigende og udviklende element. Dette glder da ikke blot for Sivards saga, men ogs for Ragnar Lodbroks historie, for s vidt den fra frst er bleven til i England. P den anden side m vi ikke alene regne med, at Nordengland er en aflgger af norsk sagakultur; den er tillige en banebryder for dens rigere udvikling. Vi har set det med dragekampen, der optages vsenlig fra engelske forestillinger, og som vistnok ad den vej finder ind i de norsk-islandske ventyrsagaer og historiske traditioner".[42]

With the situation thus before us—namely: 1. the numerical strength of the Danes and Norwegians in the north of England, which had become a second home of Norwegian saga-culture; 2. the fact that the *Hrlfssaga* was known in England, where Bjarki received the addition "Bothvar" to his name; and 3. the fact that the Siward saga as we find it in Langebek was developed in the same locality—it is evident that it was not only possible, but practically inevitable, that the *Hrlfssaga* and the Siward saga should come in contact with each other. And this was, indeed, the case. That a popular hero is said to have descended from a bear is a very widespread motive, not at all confined to the territory in which the Bjarki story was known; but the similarities in the genealogies of Siward, Bothvar Bjarki, and Ulf *(Gest. Dan.*, tenth book) are so great that the casual reader immediately concludes that these genealogies must in some way be related. Olrik has unraveled the skein and shown that the bear-ancestry belonged originally to Siward and from him was transferred to Ulf and Bjarki.

Olrik dwells on the fact that, "Det sagn, der her optrder som knyttet til historiske eller rettere halvhistoriske personer, findes ogs rundt omkring i Europas ventyr som indledning til fortllingen om den strke kmpe, der hentede de bortfrte kongedtre tilbage fra troldene." Olrik says further: "Men ogs i den islandske saga-verden har vi tilknytning. Beorn Beresuns fdsel genfindes som Bdvar Bjarkes. Bdvars forldre er den til bjrn omskabte kongesn Bjrn og bondedatteren Bera. Foruden ved navnene rbes sammenhngen ved at bjrnen—ligesom i Sakses sagn—bliver jaget og drbt, og snnen senere tager hvn. Men samtidig er motivet udviklet langt rigere, idet omskabelse og stemoder er blandet ind, og arven efter vilddyret fordeles paa tre snner: dels bjrneagtigt ydre, dels styrke og 'hamram'-hed, Sledes er de danske og de (norsk-) islandske tilknytninger af forskellig art; de danske giver os de ventyragtige elementer, hvoraf sagnet opstr. Den islandske *Hrlfssaga* og *Bjarkarmur* viser os dets videre udvikling til ventyrsaga. Selve den nordengelske Sivardssaga str i midten som et mrkeligt mellemled i udviklingen".[43] Here we have the first indication of contact between the Siward saga and the story of Bjarki, in the *Hrlfssaga*.

There is much in the main features of the lives of Siward and Bjarki that is similar. Both were men of extraordinary prowess and bravery; both gave up a great heritage at home (Siward, an earldom; Bjarki, a kingdom); both left their native land to enter the service of a foreign monarch (Siward entering the service of Edward the Confessor; Bjarki, that of Hrolf Kraki); both slew a ferocious monster; both paused in another land (Siward, on the Orkney Islands; Bjarki, in Sweden) before reaching what was to be their destination; both displayed their warlike qualities by slaying a man of great prominence who was closely connected with the king (Siward slaying Tosti, and Bjarki slaying Agnar); both were the king's chief support in his wars against his enemies; and both invaded a foreign land (Siward making an expedition to Scotland, and Bjarki accompanying Hrolf on his expedition to Sweden).

Certain features of the life of Bjarki mentioned above, such as his bravery, strength, his being in the service of Hrolf Kraki, his killing a fierce beast, and slaying Agnar, the saga-man found ready to his hand; but not the renunciation of his kingdom. Earldoms and kingdoms are not renounced "for light and transient causes." As regards Siward, who renounced his earldom, he seemed to be destined for a greater career, as subsequent events show and as is indicated by the fact that Odin (for the old man on the hill whom Siward met was none other than Odin) took a hand in directing his course. But when Bjarki renounced his kingdom, it was altogether unmotivated. The saga says: "Soon afterwards [i.e., after Bjarki's revenge on his evil stepmother] King Hring fell sick and died, whereupon Bothvar succeeded to the throne and was for a time satisfied. Later, he called his subjects together to a 'ing' [i.e., assembly] and said he wished to leave the country, married his mother to a man named Valsleit, who had been an earl, celebrated their wedding, and departed".[44] He became Hrolf's most noted warrior, but neither sought nor attained to any other distinction. The renunciation of a kingdom for the fate of a man who appears among strangers and gets what his own right arm can win for him is a rare occurrence; and when the saga-man lets Bjarki become a king and then, without reason, renounce this highest of all earthly dignities, it can only be in servile imitation of the corresponding feature of the Siward saga.

Besides those already mentioned, the two stories have other features in common. It is said of Siward, that when he learned that his son Osbeorn had fallen in battle, he became so angry that he sank his sword into a rock. It is said of Elgfrothi, Bjarki's brother, that he swung his sword against a rock with such force that it sank in to the hilt. But Elgfrothi's feat was performed under such widely different circumstances that the author may, or may not, have had Siward's feat in mind in recording the incident. However, suggestions received from one story are often employed in another quite as the author sees fit, so that, although one is not inclined to attach much importance to this incident, it is, nevertheless, worth noting.

Somewhat more noteworthy than the incident just mentioned is the introduction of Odin in both stories in the disguise of an old man. In the Siward story he appears on a hill as Siward reaches Northumberland on his journey from the Orkney Islands, and tells Siward what course to pursue, presents him the banner Ravenlandeye, which is accepted, and predicts for him a brilliant future. In the *Hrlfssaga* Odin appears as a one-eyed old man living in a hut in Sweden. Hrolf and his men seek a night's entertainment of him while on their way to the Swedish court, and the old man tests their endurance and instructs Hrolf in regard to the measures he must take to accomplish his purpose. Odin also appears to the men as they return on their way to Denmark, when he offers Hrolf a sword, shield, and armor. Hrolf declines the preferred gift, whereupon Odin tells Hrolf that he is not as wise as he thinks he is, and Hrolf soon, but too late, realizes that the rejection of the gift augurs ill fortune.

There is nothing unusual in the appearance of Odin as a one-eyed old man, for it is a common characteristic of saga literature. But though Hrolf's expedition to Sweden is mentioned in *Snorri's Edda*,[45] where the passage concerned is based on the old *Skj[o.]ldumgasaga*, the oldest authority in regard to the matter, but unfortunately now lost, no mention of Odin is made in this connection.[46] Furthermore, Odin again appears in the saga (at the close), where Bjarki vows that if he could get his eye on the god he would use him roughly for permitting the enemy to gain the victory in the battle that is being fought and that is going against Hrolf and his men. In the latter instance, Odin belongs originally to the story (*Gest. Dan.*, second book, where Odin is represented as riding his steed Sleipnir and being invisibly present at the battle to take the dead to Valhalla). The two conceptions of Odin—on the one hand as appearing in the disguise of an old man; on the other, as riding his horse, Sleipnir, and taking those fallen in battle to Valhalla—are quite different, the former being distinctly Norwegian, one of the circumstances that Olrik uses to show that the Siward saga originated under strong Norwegian influence, while the latter was the conception of Odin current in Denmark and Sweden.[47] As already stated the introduction of Odin as an old man is a motive that occurs frequently in saga literature. It cannot, therefore, be stated definitely that his appearance in the Siward saga suggested the use of him in the Bjarki story. But the two stories were current in the same locality; they were formed under similar conceptions of saga literature; in both stories Odin directs the hero in question as to the most advisable course to pursue and offers him a present; the Bjarki story already contained an instance, of another mintage, of the Odin motive; as stated above, the oldest authority in regard to the matter says nothing about Odin's appearing to Hrolf on the expedition to Sweden; and, as we know, the one has acquired important features (Bjarki's bear-ancestry and his renunciation of his kingdom) from the other. These circumstances render it highly probable that this is another of the Bjarki story's acquisitions from contact with the Siward saga. Incidents of this kind need not necessarily be used in one story as they are in another; saga literature abounds in evidence of this fact, as, for instance, Saxo's and the *Hrlfssaga's* story of Hroar and Helgi, considered later.

A feature of the *Hrlfssaga* that is much more noteworthy in this connection and that has certainly been acquired from the Siward saga is that concerning the kind of monster slain by Bjarki at the court of Hrolf Kraki. When Siward's bear-ancestry had been transferred to Bothvar Bjarki, it followed as a matter of course that Bjarki must no longer be represented as killing a bear. Siward had driven a dragon, which had killed men and cattle in great numbers, from one of the Orkney Islands; and it is in imitation of this exploit that Bjarki is represented as having slain a winged monster (dragon). This would be only another instance, in addition to those already mentioned, of the influence exerted by the story of Siward on the *Hrlfssaga*. Ordinarily, there was nothing about Bjarki's person that revealed or suggested that his father was a bear; but he was able to assume the shape of a bear, which, according to the *Hrlfssaga*, he did with terrible effect in the last battle of Hrolf and his warriors. Since he sustained such near relationship to the bear-family, it would be inappropriate to represent him as showing his prowess by killing a bear, for his sentiments toward that animal would, as a result of his own ancestry and the treatment his father had received, be those of sympathy rather than antipathy. His mother had told him the whole story of his ancestry and the maltreatment of his father, and it had aroused him to take most dire revenge. Consequently, he must be represented as having killed some other kind of ferocious beast, or monster, than a bear, and this naturally became the same kind of monster that Siward had overcome, namely a dragon. The fact that it was not uncommon at the time the saga was composed for a popular hero to be represented as having slain a dragon made it all the easier for the author of the *Hrlfssaga* to imitate this feature of the Siward saga. It may be said that this is attributing too much consistency in one particular to a story that otherwise is a piece of patch-work. But the story of Bjarki's fight with the winged monster is not patch-work; it does not represent the poorest and latest form of the Bjarki legends, as Olrik says;[48] it is not an impossible story, as Panzer says;[49] nor is it "inconsequent and absurd," as Lawrence says.[50] Considering the time at which it was written, it is a well considered, well constructed narrative, in which the material at hand and the machinery that was regarded as permissible and appropriate in saga-writing at the time is employed with great skill to produce the intended effect. The story is as follows:—

"Ok sem lei at jlum, geruz menn ktir. B[o.]varr spyrr H[o.]tt, hverju etta stti; hann segir honum, at dr eitt hafi ar komit tv vetr samt, mikit og gurligt—'ok hefir vngi bakinu ok flgr at jafnan; tvau haust hefir at n hingat vitjat ok gert mikinn skaa; at bta ekki vpn, en kappar konungs koma ekki heim, eir sem at eru einna mestir.' B[o.]varr mlti: 'ekki er h[o.]llin sv vel skipu, sem ek tlai, ef eitt dr skal hr eya rki og f konungsins.' H[o.]ttr sagi: 'at er ekki dr, heldr er at hit mesta tr[o.]ll.' N kemr jlaaptann; , mlti konungr: 'n vil ek, at menn s kyrrir ok hljir ntt, ok banna ek [o.]llum mnum m[o.]nnum at ganga n[o.]kkurn hska vi drit, en f ferr eptir v sem aunar; menn mna vil ek ekki missa.' Allir heita hr gu um, at gera eptir v, sem konungr bau. B[o.]varr leyndiz burt um nttina; hann ltr H[o.]tt fara me sr, ok gerir hann at nauugr ok kallai hann sr strt til bana. B[o.]varr segir, at betr mundi til takaz. eir ganga burt fr h[o.]llinni, ok verr B[o.]varr at bera hann; sv er hann hrddr. N sj eir drit; ok v nst pir H[o.]ttr slkt, sem hann m, ok kva drit mundu gleypa hann. B[o.]varr ba bikkjuna hans egja ok kastar honum nir mosann, ok ar liggr hann ok eigi me [o.]llu hrddr; eigi orir hann heim at fara heldr. N gengr B[o.]varr mti drinu; at hfir honum, at sverit er fast umgj[o.]rinni, er hann vildi brega v. B[o.]varr eggjar n fast sverit ok bragar umgj[o.]rinni, ok n fr hann brugit umgj[o.]rinni, sv, *at* sverit gengr r slirunum, ok leggr egar undir bgi drsins ok sv fast, at st hjartanu, ok datt drit til jarar dautt nir. Eptir at ferr hann angat sem H[o.]ttr liggr. B[o.]varr tekr hann upp ok berr angat, sem drit liggr dautt. H[o.]ttr skelfr kaft. B[o.]varr mlti: 'n skaltu drekka bl drsins.' Hann er lengi tregr, en orir hann vst eigi annat. B[o.]varr ltr hann drekka tv sopa stra; hann lt hann ok eta n[o.]kkut af drshjartanu; eptir etta tekr B[o.]varr til hans, ok ttuz eir vi lengi. B[o.]varr mlti: 'helzt ertu n sterkr orinn, ok ekki vnti ek, at hriz n hirmenn Hrlfs konungs.' H[o.]ttr sagi: 'eigi mun ek hraz ok eigi ik upp fr, essu.' 'Vel er orit, H[o.]ttr flagi; f[o.]ru vit n til ok reisum upp drit ok bum sv um, at arir tli at kvikt muni vera.' eir gera n sv. Eptir at fara eir heim ok hafa kyrt um sik, ok veit engi mar, hvat eir hafa ijat. Konungr spyrr um morguninn, nvat eir viti til drsins, hvrt at hafi n[o.]kkut angat vitjat um nttina; honum var sagt, at f alt vri heilt grindum ok sakat. Konungr ba menn forvitnaz, hvrt engi si lkindi til, at at hefi heim komit. Varmenn geru sv ok kmu skjtt aptr ok sogu konungi, at drit fri ar ok heldr geyst at borginni. Konungr ba hirmenn vera hrausta ok duga n hvern eptir v, sem hann hefi hug til, ok ra af vtt enna; ok sv var gert, sem konungr bau, at eir bjuggu sik til ess.

Konungr horfi drit ok mlti san: 'enga s ek f[o.]r drinu, en hverr vill n taka kaup einn ok ganga mti v?' B[o.]varr mlti: 'at vri nsta hraustsmanns forvitnisbt. H[o.]ttr flagi, rektu n af er illmlit at, at menn lta, sem engi krellr n dugr muni r vera; far n ok drep drit; mttu sj, at engi er allfss til annarra.' 'J, sagi H[o.]ttr, ek mun til essa raz.' Konungr mlti: 'ekki veit ek, hvaan essi hreysti er at r komin, H[o.]ttr, ok mikit hefir um ik skipaz , skammri stundu.' H[o.]ttr mlti: 'gef mr til sverit Gullinhjalta, er heldr , ok skal ek fella drit ea f bana.' Hrlfr konungr mlti: 'etta sver er ekki beranda nema eim manni, sem bi er gr drengr og hraustr.' H[o.]ttr sagi: 'sv skaltu til tla, at mr s sv httat.' Konungr mlti: 'hvat m vita, nema fleira hafi skipz um hagi na, en sj ykkir, en fstir menn ykkjaz ik kenna, at, sr enn sami mar; n tak vi sverinu ok njt manna bezt, ef etta er til unnit.' San gengr H[o.]ttr at drinu alldjarfliga ok hggr til ess, , *er* hann kemr h[o.]ggfri, ok drit fellr nir dautt. B[o.]varr mlti: 'sji n, herra, hvat hann hefir til unnit.' Konungr segir: 'vst hefir hann mikit skipaz, en ekki hefir H[o.]ttr einn drit drepit, heldr hefir at gert.' B[o.]varr segir: 'vera m, at sv s.' Konungr segir: 'vissa ek, *er* komt hr, at fir mundu nir jafningjar vera, en at ykki mr itt verk frgiligast, at hefir gert hr annan kappa, ar *er* H[o.]ttr er, ok vnligr tti til mikillar giptu; ok n vil ek *at* hann heiti eigi H[o.]ttr lengr ok skal hann heita Hjalti upp fr essu; skaltu heita eptir sverinu Gullinhjalta'".[51]

The consistency observed in displacing the bear, as the animal killed by Bjarki has been noted, as has also the reason why the dragon was introduced as a substitute for the bear. It will be observed that the account of the dragon in the Siward story suggested the further development of the story in the *Hrlfssaga*. Olrik says: "I n henseende bar Sivard den digres kamp dog noget eget. De almindelige norrne dragekampe lige fra Sigurds drab p Fvne har stadig til ml at vinde dragens guld. For Sivard digre eksisterer dette motiv ikke; han vil frelse de hjemsgte mennesker. Af alle de islandske dragekampe har kun Bjrn Hitdlekmpes noget tilsvarende, og her er det nppe tilfldigt at ogs den er henlagt til de engelske farvande. Det er det engelske dragekamps-motiv".[52] Olrik further calls attention to the fact that in English tales the object is not to kill the dragon, but to drive it away, as Siward did. But to fit the dragon into the Bjarki story, it had to be killed in order that the blood-drinking episode might be introduced. This involved no difficulty, however; for the killing of the dragon was in harmony with Scandinavian saga-usage. But it should be observed how, in essence, the conception of the dragon in the Bjarki story harmonizes accurately with that in the Siward story. The king and his court are afflicted by the visitations of a dragon; and Bjarki puts an end to this affliction by killing the dragon, as Siward, in the corresponding situation, does by driving it away.

Not less terrible than dragons, but much more common, were trolls; and this fact led Brynjulfsson to remark that the introduction of a troll in this connection was as characteristic as anything could be.[53] The introduction of the troll is quite in harmony with the genius of Old Norse folk-lore. The saga-man did not, however, characterize the dragon as a troll merely because he would thus be employing good saga-material, but because the depredations ascribed to the dragon in the Siward story, which were quite foreign to the accounts of dragons in Scandinavian folk-lore, were very suggestive of the depredations ascribed to trolls, and because a troll story would enable him to work out his plot with admirable effect. The statement in the saga, "As the Yule-feast approached, the men grew depressed," is a characteristic beginning of a troll story; for, while trolls commit their depredations at all times of the year and under a multitude of circumstances, many of the stories about them begin with such expressions as: "Yule was approaching. On the eve the shepherd went with his sheep";[54] "In old days no one could stay over Christmas Eve";[55] "It happened once late on a Yule Eve";[56] "Formerly every Christmas Eve";[57] "I gamle dage var det en julenat";[58] "Juleaften gik Per Bakken til kvernhuset";[59] "Nogen av selskapet kom til at tale on Hammertrollet, som det nu kaltes, og de mente, at skulde de nogengang vente ulempe av det arrige troll, saa maatte det vel vasre saadan i julegryet".[60]

Thus, as we see, the statement that the winged monster appears late Christmas Eve,[61] is exactly in harmony with the belief, still current in some parts of Norway, that on Christmas Eve, after sunset, but never earlier in the day, an adventure with a troll is to be expected unless proper precaution be taken to avoid it. It is a part of the superstition, that if any one ventures into, or near, the stable or other outbuildings late in the evening, he is in the greatest danger of being attacked by one of these malignant beings; and people are in mortal terror of falling into the clutches of a troll. As a result, there is great haste to get the chores done up early on Christmas Eve. In fact, the fear that Hott shows before leaving the hall, when he knows he must go out, and the extreme fear that he shows later, can be duplicated from the tales that are told in connection with the superstition. There is no danger, however, so long as one remains in the house.[62]

A story, pertinent in this connection, is told to illustrate the difficulties that ministers in the rural districts in Norway have had to contend with on account of the superstitious belief in trolls. A minister had exerted himself to root out of the people in his parish the belief in trolls. Among those whom he had endeavored to enlighten was a boy. But so ingrained had this belief become in the boy that, when Christmas Eve arrived and he was requested to go to one of the outbuildings on an errand, he was seized with fright. He went on the errand, however, and performed it without seeing a troll; but on his return he was so overcome with the fear that a troll was pursuing him that he fell to the ground, and had to be met by people from the house and escorted back.[63] The story is supposed to be true, and there is no reason to doubt it. But whether it is true or not is immaterial in this connection; in any event, it shows what kind of story we are dealing with in the saga, and it shows to what admirable use the story enabled the saga-man to put the inordinate fear and cowardice of Hott. In view of the circumstances (Hott's cowardice and the common fear of the Christmas troll), Hott's actions, when he is forced to accompany Bjarki and when he sees the monster, are perfectly natural; and to see the matter in any other light is not to understand the story.

Another feature of the first part of the story that should be noticed is the dual nature of the monster. A dragon was as terrible a creature as one could imagine; a troll was also as terrible a creature as one could imagine. But the saga-man has introduced into his story a being that combines the characteristics of both. Hott knew that the monster possessed this dual nature, for it is from him that the author lets the statement proceed, "That is no beast, it is rather the greatest troll." This makes it still more natural for him to display ridiculous fear. It also explains the king's fear of the monster, and removes the odium that might seem to attach to the king and his warriors in withdrawing from a combat with such a creature and allowing it, unopposed, to perform its Yule-tide depredations and depart. The saga-man did not intend to be-little Hrolf Kraki; he intended to magnify Bjarki by introducing a monster for him to overcome that it was no shame for other mortals to avoid. Nor is it accidental that the reader is informed of the troll-nature of the dragon in a statement made by Hott to Bjarki. It serves to make it plain that Bjarki also knew what kind of monster the dragon was. This places in the strongest relief his courage in undertaking voluntarily, nay against the express command of the king, to attack the beast, and his prowess in felling it without difficulty. What single feat could he have performed, or in what manner could he have performed it, to reflect greater credit on himself? The cowardly Hott he had to have with him also, in order that the blood-drinking episode might be introduced; but Hott's childish actions encumbered him at a time when they would be very provoking and it might be necessary for Bjarki to have command of all his resources to gain a victory.

In the scene that follows the slaying of the dragon, it seems at first sight that an incongruous element has been introduced. That Hott is compelled to eat some of the dragon's heart is good saga-material, as is evident from the similar episode in the *Volsungasaga* (i.e., Sigurd's eating some of Favnir's heart); but the dragon is also a troll, and there is no sanction in saga-literature for eating a troll's heart and drinking a troll's blood to gain strength and courage. Trolls have always been regarded as detestable beings; and in drinking the blood of a troll, it might seem that one would acquire detestable qualities. But, on the one hand, the difficulty, if indeed story-tellers of the time regarded the matter as presenting a difficulty, was unavoidable without a reconstruction of the whole story; on the other hand, so far as the monster was a dragon, no difficulty would be involved, and so far as the monster had the nature of a troll, the heart-eating and blood-drinking would certainly be regarded as imparting strength. In such scenes as this it is never the intention that one who eats the heart of a dragon or drinks an animal's blood shall acquire all the characteristics of the animal; every scene of this kind would then be ridiculous from any point of view. The eating and drinking are done to gain strength and courage, as is the case here; and it is not proper to subject this scene to a more critical judgment than similar scenes in other sagas. The strength of a troll was certainly not to be despised; and we find this particular episode sanctioned in a way in the *Bjarkarmur*, where it is said that after Hjalti had drunk of the blood of the wolf, he became, not as strong as a wolf, but "as strong as a troll." In view of the fact that the troll is a troll-dragon, that the eating of its heart associates the episode very closely with the similar episode in the *Volsungasaga*, and that the *rmur* magnify Hjalti's strength by saying that it is equal to that of a troll, it is hypercritical to say that the saga here contains an incongruous element. And however insistent one may be in maintaining that the author has introduced an element that is not recognized saga-material, it must be admitted that he has so skillfully fused it with good saga-material that it is not probable, as the *rmur* show, that contemporary readers found any fault with the episode.

But does such a monster as a troll-dragon have any sanction in folk-lore? Yes, it does. It is characteristic of Norse folk-lore to ascribe troll-like qualities to beings about which there seems to be something supernatural, such as invulnerability. In one of Asbjrnsen's tales, there is a story about a troll-bird, told by a man named Per Sandaker, who "was supposed to be strong in stories about troll-birds." In the story referred to, there is a woodgrouse (tiur) which has become known as a fabulous animal (fabeldyr) throughout the whole neighborhood. "One might just as well shoot at a stone,' said Per, with the greatest conviction"; for he had shot at the bird and made the feathers fly, without being able to injure it. Later, on the hunting-trip on which Per was telling about the bird, he and a companion came across it. "Now he is out again, the old fellow," said Per; "there is no use in the wide world to shoot at him, one might just as well shoot at the clouds." The men maneuvered for a position; and Per's companion, who is telling the story, says, "My gun was raised, and the mighty bird tumbled down head first." Per picked it up and examined it and declared that it was the troll-bird; he could tell it by the beak. On the same trip stories were told about troll-hares that for a time had escaped uninjured but had finally been killed.[64]

Panzer[65] and others have called attention to the discrepancy between the statement that the monster in the saga is said to be invulnerable, and that it is nevertheless killed. In the story from Asbjrnsen's tales we have the explanation. The troll-animal seems to be invulnerable until some one appears who has the requisite skill or strength, or a combination of both, to dispatch it; and it might be observed that Bjarki paid no more attention to Hott's statement about the invulnerability of the troll-dragon than Per's companion paid to Per's statement about the invulnerability of the troll-bird.

Finnur Jnsson calls the dragon a hall-attacking monster;[66] but this appellation is hardly correct. The only thing in the saga might fairly suggest it is Bjarki's statement, "The hall isn't so well defended as I thought, if a beast can destroy the domain and property of the king." But Hott has not said that the monster had attached the hall; and if it be insisted that it is the author who has presented Bjarki as making the statement and has not paused to weigh nicely the dramatic proprieties, the reply may be made that Bjarki thinks of how weakly the king's hall is defended when a monster can regularly defy his men and come off without injury. He does not imply that the hall has been attacked; he refers to the destruction of "the domain and property of the king." In any event, the saga does not represent the monster as attacking the hall. To continue immediately after the statement just quoted: Hott answered, 'That is no beast, it is rather the greatest troll.' Now came the Yule-even; and the king said, 'Now I desire that all the men be still and quiet in the night, and I forbid them all to run any risk on account of the beast; let the cattle fare as fate wills; my men I do not wish to lose'. The king expects the cattle to fare ill, but wishes to run no risk of losing his men; however, if they remain in the hall in the night, there will be no risk of losing them, because (such is the necessary conclusion) the hall and the men in the hall will not be attacked. Hence, the monster cannot be called a hall-attacking monster; it is a cattle-attacking monster. Again, Bjarki did not expect the monster to attack the hall. If he had, he would probably have done as Beowulf did under similar circumstances—awaited its arrival. And the king's men did not expect the monster to attack the hall, for they seem to have gone to sleep; this is implied in the statement telling about Bjarki's and Hott's return to the hall, "Then they went in and were quiet; no one knew what they had done." If the men had been on guard for the monster, which was the only rational thing for them to do if they expected the hall to be attacked, the opportunity for Bjarki and Hott to sneak out, remain some length of time, and return, all unobserved, would have been cut off. Later, after Bjarki had crept out at night and killed the dragon, compelling Hott to go with him, *etc.*, the saga continues, "The king asked in the morning whether they knew anything of the beast; whether it had showed itself anywhere in the night; they told him the cattle were all safe and sound in the folds." From this it follows that the dragon might have appeared and killed all the cattle, so far as the king knew; he had paid no attention to the matter in the night; he had apparently been asleep. The question was not whether the monster had attacked the hall; it was not expected to attack the hall; and the fact that it had not attacked the hall signified nothing as to whether it had made its appearance. The question was whether the cattle had suffered; and when the king asked if the beast "had showed itself anywhere in the night," the answer was that "the cattle were all safe and sound in the folds." The extreme danger to which the cattle were exposed, and the entire safety of the men if they remained in the hall during the night, show again that this was no hall-attacking monster, but "et kongsgrden hjemsgende uhyre," a troll that destroyed cattle and did not endanger the men unless they left the hall in the night and exposed themselves to attack.

Among the Icelandic legends collected by Jn Arnason is a story which, in certain important particulars, is very much like the story about Bjarki's fight with the troll-dragon. A portion of it is as follows:—

"A man named Gudmundur lived once upon a time at a farm called Silfrnarstadir, in the bay of Skagafjrdur. He was very rich in flocks, and looked upon by his neighbours as a man of high esteem and respectability. He was married, but had no children.

"It happened one Christmas Eve, at Silfrnarstadir, that the herdsman did not return home at night, and, as he was not found at the sheep-pens, the farmer caused a diligent search to be made for him all over the country, but quite in vain.

"Next spring Gudmundur hired another shepherd, named Grmur, who was tall and strong, and boasted of being able to resist anybody. But the farmer, in spite of the man's boldness and strength, warned him to be careful how he ran risks, and on Christmas Eve bade him drive the sheep early into the pens, and come home to the farm while it was still daylight. But in the evening Grmur did not come, and though search was made far and near for him, was never found. People made all sorts of guesses about the cause of his disappearance, but the farmer was full of grief, and after this could not get any one to act as shepherd for him.

"At this time there lived a poor widow at Sjvarborg, who had several children, of whom the eldest, aged fourteen years, was named Sigurdur.

"To this woman the farmer at last applied, and offered her a large sum of money if she would allow her son to act as shepherd for him. Sigurdur was very anxious that his mother should have all this money, and declared himself most willing to undertake the office; so he went with the farmer, and during the summer was most successful in his new situation, and never lost a sheep.

"At the end of a certain time the farmer gave Sigurdur a wether, a ewe, and a lamb as a present, with which the youth was much pleased.

"Gudmundur became much attached to him, and on Christmas Eve begged him to come home from his sheep before sunset.

"All day long the boy watched the sheep, and when evening approached, he heard the sound of heavy footsteps on the mountains Turning around he saw coming towards him a gigantic and terrible troll.

"She addressed him, saying, 'Good evening, my Sigurdur. I am come to put you into my bag.'

"Sigurdur answered, 'Are you cracked? Do you not see how thin I am? Surely I am not worth your notice. But I have a sheep and fat lamb here which I will give you for your pot this evening.'

"So he gave her the sheep and the lamb, which she threw on her shoulder, and carried off up the mountain again. Then Sigurdur went home, and right glad was the farmer to see him safe, and asked him whether he had seen anything.

"'Nothing whatever, out of the common,' replied the boy.

"After New Year's day the farmer visited the flock, and, on looking them over, missed the sheep and lamb which he had given the youth, and asked him what had become of them. The boy answered that a fox had killed the lamb, and that the wether had fallen into a bog; adding, 'I fancy I shall not be very lucky with *my* sheep.'

> "When he heard this, the farmer gave him one ewe and two wethers, and asked him to remain another year in his service. Sigurdur consented to do so.
>
> "Next Christmas Eve, Gudmundur begged Sigurdur to be cautious, and not run any risks, for he loved him as his own son.
>
> "But the boy answered, 'You need not fear, there are no risks to run.'"

The troll appeared again, and Sigurdur gave her two old and two young sheep. When he returned to the farm he declared that he had seen nothing unusual. Next year the troll appeared as usual, and took four sheep, which Sigurdur offered her, and himself besides. When she arrived at her cave, she bade Sigurdur kill them, and then bade him sharpen an axe, for she was going kill him. He did so, but she spared him.

From this point, the story becomes more of a common fairy tale. By following the troll's advice, Sigurdur won Margaret, the dean's daughter.[67]

This is another story about a troll that comes on Christmas Eve and harms people only when they expose themselves after sunset. Particularly noteworthy are the statements: "Gudmundur became attached to him, and on Christmas Eve begged him to come home from his sheep before sunset";—"Next Christmas Eve, Gudmundur begged Sigurdur to be cautious, and not run any risks, for he loved him as his own son";—and, "The farmer ... asked him whether he had seen anything. 'Nothing whatever, out of the common,' replied the boy." They bear a striking resemblance to the corresponding statements in the *Hrlfssaga*: "The king said, 'Now I desire that all the men be still and quiet in the night, and I forbid them all to run any risk on account of the beast; let the cattle fare as fate wills; my men I do not wish to lose'";—and, "The king asked in the morning whether they knew anything of the beast; whether it had showed itself anywhere in the night; they told him the cattle were all safe and sound in the folds."

The purpose of calling attention to the story in Arnason's collection is that it may aid in showing what kind of story the dragon story in the saga really is. That the most terrible kind of troll attacks the cattle[68] of the famous King Hrolf Kraki and is dispatched by the noted hero Bothvar Bjarki does not alter the nature of the story.

A possible objection remains, which should be removed. When the warders in the morning saw the dead propped-up dragon, they said "that the beast was advancing rapidly to attack the town." And "the king bade his men be courageous, [and said] each one should help, according as he had courage for it, and proceed against the monster." But it is plain that, since the beast was apparently coming in the morning, in broad daylight, instead of at night, it seemed to have changed its tactics, and no one could tell what it intended to do. It was the part of wisdom to prepare for the worst. Besides, the men would have better prospects of success, or at least of avoiding injury, in an encounter with it in daylight when its maneuvers could be watched and guarded against. That the warders in a state of excitement said that "the beast was advancing rapidly to attack the town," is of no significance. They merely expressed the thought that came to their minds; and they were palpably wrong when they said that it "was advancing rapidly." But it is an exquisite touch on the part of the saga-man to have the warders utter these words. They got one view of the monster and hastened back. Of course, the beast was advancing and advancing rapidly; it would never occur to them, unless they had paused to take note of it, which they did not do, that the monster was standing still.

It may seem that too much attention is devoted to this feature of the story. But it is important to establish, if possible, the type of story we have before us in this much discussed tale about Bjarki and the troll-dragon. Regardless of where the author got the idea of the dragon, he has made use of the popular story about the troll that comes Christmas Eve and attacks those who venture out into the open after dark. And when the saga-man transformed the story into one of this type, he did it with the conscious purpose of providing a story that would enable him to let Bjarki take Hott out secretly at night, kill the dragon, compel Hott to eat of its heart and drink of its blood, put Hott's newly acquired strength to the test, prop the dead dragon up in a living posture, thus paving the way for further developments, and then return to the hall—all unseen and without arousing a breath of suspicion. The type of story is adapted precisely to the requirements of the author's plan. That the propping-up of an animal that has been slain is good saga-material, or has the sanction of earlier usage, is admitted, and need not be dwelt upon here.

The type to which the dragon story belongs has a bearing on its relationship to the Grendel story. Grendel is a hall-attacking monster; the troll-dragon is not a hall-attacking monster. If the dragon story in the saga is a modification of the Grendel story in *Beowulf*, or if it is a modification even of the story about the fire-spewing dragon, there has been a change, not only in the details of the story and the nature of the monster, but it has been transferred from one well-defined type of story to another. There is, indeed, a type of troll story in which the troll comes Christmas Eve and attacks the inmates of the house, not the cattle in the stable or in the folds. To this type belongs the story in the *Grettissaga* in which the troll-wife attacks the man of the house[69] and which is often compared with the Grendel story. Another story of the same type is that about Per Gynt, who, having been informed that a certain house is invaded by trolls every Christmas Eve so that the inmates must seek refuge elsewhere, decides to ask for lodging there overnight next Christmas Eve in order that he may put an end to the depredations of the trolls. The trolls make their appearance as usual, and with the aid of a tame polar bear Per Gynt puts them to flight.[70] But these stories must be sharply differentiated from the Bjarki story and others of its type; so that while the Grettir story and the Grendel story are essentially of the same type, the story about the winged monster in the *Hrlfssaga* and the Grendel story are not of the same type.

The last episode in the story about Bjarki and the winged monster has met with more criticism than any other portion of it. Olrik says that the story should have given us a real test of Hjalti's manhood;[71] Lawrence says, "The beast-propping episode spoils the courage-scene";[72] and Panzer says that this part of the story is impossible, because Hjalti is represented as killing a dead monster, and Hrolf, although he perceives the deception that has been practiced, nevertheless gives the swindler the heroic name Hjalti.[73] Panzer is also inclined to make much of Hjalti's asking for, and receiving, the king's sword, as he mentions the matter twice. Once he says, "Warum er des Knigs Schwert verlangt, gibt die Saga nicht an, er 'ttet' damit das (tote) Tier wie in den *Rmur*";[74] and again, "Man sieht nicht, warum und wozu Hjalti des Knigs Schwert zu seiner Scheintat erbittet und erhlt".[75] Furthermore, Kluge, Sarrazin, Holthausen, Lawrence, and Panzer[76] would identify "gylden hilt" in *Beowulf* with Gullinhjalti in the saga.

In considering this portion of the story it should be observed that the saga-man had a fourfold purpose in view. Bjarki must receive credit for his great achievement in killing the troll-dragon; he must receive credit for having made a brave man of the cow Hott; Hott must give proof of his newly acquired courage; his change of name must also be made, and, as is most appropriate, it must result, and result naturally, from the deed by which his courage is displayed. But before proceeding to an explanation of how the author manipulates the scene so as to accomplish his purpose, let us see how he has prepared for it.

The monster is dead. Hott has partaken of its strength-giving blood and heart. Bjarki and Hott have wrestled long, so that Bjarki has brought Hott to a thorough realization of the strength he now possesses, for that is the significance of the wrestling-match; and what better assurance could Hott have that he is now very strong than that he is not put to shame in wrestling with Bjarki who has overawed the king's warriors and slain the terrible dragon? Finally, the dragon is propped up and the two retire.

The morning comes and the monster is in view; but some of the terror that its expected arrival in the darkness had inspired has disappeared when it is seen in broad daylight. An effort ought really to be made to destroy it, but the king will not command any one to take the risk involved in attacking it. He calls for a volunteer, and the fact that no one volunteers shows what the men think of it. Bjarki sees an opportunity to continue what he has begun in the night, by having Hott do what will win him the reputation and place among the king's men to which, owing to the change that he has undergone, he is now entitled; and he calls on Hott to show his strength and courage by attacking the beast. Hott knows that the monster is dead, but this is not the reason why he accedes to Bjarki's request. He realizes now that Bjarki's friendship is beyond question and that everything that Bjarki has done with regard to him, and asked him to do, has been for the best; and though he feels that he is called upon to engage m a strange proceeding, loyalty to his friend, who probably is equal to this occasion, as he has been to every other, impels him to do as requested and assist in playing the game to the end. So he says to the king, "Give me your sword Gullinhjalti, which you are bearing, and I will kill the beast or die in the attempt."

Whether Hott has a sword of his own the saga does not tell, and it is quite immaterial. That such a coward as Hott has been has no business carrying a sword, would be sufficient justification for his being without one. But whether he has a weapon or no, if he is going to attack the monster he ought to be armed with the best sword available; and whose would that be but the king's sword? If the king expects any one to run the risk of attacking the beast, he ought to be willing to do what he can to assure success in the undertaking. He feels the force of the argument implied in Hott's request, and hands him his sword; but he says, "This sword can only be borne by a man who is both brave and daring." Hott answers, "You shall be convinced that I am such a man." He then goes up to the beast and knocks it over. But a beast that has shown itself to be so terrible on former occasions cannot be alive and yet stand stock still and allow itself to be killed and tumbled over in this manner. It must have been killed before, and now the king strongly suspects that the reason why Bjarki has urged Hott to attack it was that Bjarki, having killed the monster himself, knew that it was dead; and when he is charged with the deed he does not deny it. Thus Bjarki gets the credit for his achievement.

It is true, as Mllenhoff,[77] ten Brink,[78] and Olrik[79] have said, that the main object of the whole story of Bjarki and the dragon is to motivate Hott's newly acquired courage. Bjarki compels Hott to go with him when the dragon is to be attacked; he compels him to eat and drink what will give him strength and courage; he props up the dead dragon in order that, as the sequel shows, Hott may gain the reputation of being what he now really is, a brave man; and while, of the two achievements with which Bjarki is credited, the killing of the dragon is passed over lightly, his having made a brave man of Hott is strongly emphasized. But there can be no doubt that the saga-man planned that Bjarki should get credit for killing the dragon; for Bjarki does get such credit, and it must be presumed that, what the author permits to occur, he planned should occur. It is also natural that more emphasis is laid on his having made a hero of Hott than on his having slain the monster. Now that the beast is dead, the killing of it proved not to be an impossible feat, and Bjarki has shown before, that he possesses the qualities necessary for such a deed. But that he possesses the ability to make a hero out of the miserable, cowardly wretch, Hott, is a revelation of a new and uncommon power. He has not only dispatched the king's most dangerous foe, he has added another brave man to the number of the king's retainers. This naturally attracts the king's particular attention, and he gives Bjarki special credit for the achievement.

But when Bjarki is known to have killed the beast, what becomes of Hott's display of bravery, or even the appearance of bravery? His whole demeanor, from the moment he accedes to Bjarki's request to attack the beast, reveals the change in his nature. But the proof of this change consists, not in knocking over the dragon, but in his ability to wield the sword which the king himself says can "only be borne by a man who is both brave and daring." This must be conclusive proof to the king and to all present. It is not accidental that it is the king's sword that Hott uses and that it is the king himself who makes the remark about it which he does. The king, above all men, must be convinced of Hott's bravery, and in view of the manner in which Hott's bravery is displayed, the king must, indeed, be satisfied with the proof. Thus this purpose of the scene is also accomplished. Nor has the saga-man devised an artificial method of testing strength and courage. It is quite in harmony with folk-lore. That a strength-giving drink enables one to wield a sword that an ordinary mortal cannot handle, is a motive employed in a number of fairy tales. It occurs, for instance, in *Soria Moria Castle*, one of the best known Norse fairy tales. It is told that Halvor, a typical good-for-nothing fellow and groveler-in-the-ashes, has arrived at a castle inhabited by a princess and a three-headed troll. The princess warns Halvor to beware of the monster, but he decides to await the troll's arrival. Halvor is hungry and asks for meat to eat. "When Halvor had eaten his fill, the princess told him to try if he could brandish the sword that hung against the wall; no, he couldn't brandish it—he couldn't even lift it up. 'Oh,' said the princess, 'now you must go and take a pull of that flask that hangs by its side; that's what the troll does every time he goes out to use the sword.' So Halvor took a pull, and in a twinkling of an eye he could brandish the sword like anything".[80] It is apparent, therefore, that the saga-man intend Hott's ability to wield the king's sword to constitute the proof of his bravery. Thus the author's third purpose is accomplished, and the king rewards Hott, not in spite of the deception that been practiced and revealed, but on account of his bravery, which been proved.[81]

In Saxon, Hjalti has no other name than "Hialto." In the *Hrlfssaga* he first has the name "Hott" and this is changed to "Hjalti." The appropriate time for changing it is, as has been said, when his change of nature becomes apparent; and his new name is most fittingly derived from the deed by which he manifests that he has become a different man from what he was. "Hjalti" means "hilt"; hence, he must get his name from a hilt; but it should come from the hilt of a sword connected with his display of courage, and this is the king's sword. It is a fine conception that, as Hjalti gets his new name from his ability to wield the wonderful sword of the king, his name is a constant reminder of his bravery. But the name of the king's sword is Skofnung; hence, as the word has no suggestion of "hilt" in it, it is not available in this connection. The form "hjalti" must appear in some way to suggest the name; and since the name is to come from the king's sword the word "hjalti" must be used in connection with it. But what kind of hilt would the king's sword naturally have? A golden hilt, of course. So far as the words are concerned, "iron hilt," "brass hilt," or "silver hilt" would have served the purpose just as well, had it been appropriate to use any of these terms. But the king's sword must have a golden hilt. Hence, Hott says to the king, "Give me your sword Gullinhjalti, which you are bearing, and I will kill the beast." And after the king is convinced of Hott's bravery he says, "And now I wish him called Hott no longer, he shall from this day be named Hjalti,—thou shalt be called after the sword Gullinhjalti." Thus Hjalti gets his name from the king's sword; and this, again, is proof that it is by wielding the king's sword that Hjalti displays his courage. That "Gullinhjalti" is written as one word and capitalized may be a late development and signify no more than the modern treatment by some writers of "gylden hilt" (i.e., writing it "Gyldenhilt") in *Beowulf.* Even if we assume that the original author of the word intended "Gullinhjalti" as a proper noun and the name of the king's sword, it does not necessarily conflict with the idea that the name of the king's sword is Skofnung. "Gullinhjalti" would then be a by-name, a pet-name, for Skofnung, derived from its golden hilt. It can hardly be presumed that when the saga-man in this connection calls the king's sword "Gullinhjalti," he has for the moment forgotten that the name of Hrolf's famous sword is Skofnung. Nor is it in conflict with the description of Skofnung that Gullinhjalti is given a supernatural quality. Skofnung also has a supernatural quality. It is Skofnung's nature to utter a loud sound whenever it reaches the bone.[82]

That two swords in two widely separated compositions are identical requires more proof than that the term "golden hilt" is used in connection with both of them; and in the two compositions in question there is nothing else than this term, and the peculiarity of the one sword that it can be wielded only by a man of unusual strength, of the other that it can be wielded only by a brave man, on which to base an identity. The fact of the matter is that it is the requirement of the plot that has supplied both the name and the unusual quality of the sword Gullinhjalti in the *Hrlfssaga*. Other requirements would have produced other results.

But since such stress has been laid on the similarity between "gylden hilt" (*Beowulf*) and "Gullinhjalti" (*Hrlfssaga*) in the attempt to identify Bothvar Bjarki with Beowulf, let us turn our attention, before proceeding further, to the portion of *Beowulf* where the term "gylden hilt" occurs.

The text shows clearly that the author of *Beowulf* did not intend "gylden hilt" as a proper noun. He never uses the word "hilt" in connection with the weapon in question to designate the sword as a whole. "Hilt," both as a simple word and in compounds, is used only to designate the handle of the sword. The following terms are used for the sword as a whole: "bil,"[83] "sweord,"[84] "w[=]pen,"[85] "m[=]l,"[86] "[=i]rena cyst."[87] The word "hilt" is used seven times. Sarrazin says, "Es ist bemerkenswert, dass bei jenem Schwert, auch als es noch vollstndig und unversehrt war, regelmssig die hilze, der griff (hilt), hervorgehoben wurde (ll. 1563, 1574, 1614, 1668, 1677, 1687, 1698)."[88] But the statements, "H[=e] gef[=e][=i]ng [=a] fetel-hilt,"[89] "W[=]pen hafenade heard be hiltum,"[90] contain the only two instances in which the hilt is mentioned before the blade melted. It is quite natural for the author to say, "He then seized the belted hilt," "The strong man raised the sword by the hilt"; for the hilt is the part of the weapon that is intended to be held in the hand when a sword is to be used. It is hardly correct to say that the hilt is here emphasized.

"Ne n[=o]m h[=e] [=i]n [=]m w[=i]cum, Weder-G[=e]ata l[=e]od, m[=a]m-[=]hta m[=a], [=e]h h[=e] [=]r monige geseah, b[=u]ton one hafelan ond [=a] hilt somod, since f[=a]ge; sweord [=]r gemealt."[91]

"Hilt" does not here mean "sword," because "sweord [=]r gemealt" and nothing but the hilt was left to be taken away. The same applies to "hilt" in the statement, "Ic t hilt anan f[=e]ondum tferede."[92]

"[=a] ws gylden hilt gamelum rince,
h[=a]rum hild-fruman, on hand gyfen,
enta [=]r-geweorc."[93]

In this passage, "hilt" cannot refer to the whole sword, because the blade had melted; only the hilt remained. To say that the hilt was given to the king, was proper, for (making allowance, of course, for the fictional nature of the whole story) it was literally true; but to say that "Gyldenhilt" (the sword) was given to the king, would not be proper, because the principal part of the sword had disappeared. The word "gylden" is used in this passage apparently for two reasons: 1. that the hilt is of gold renders it more appropriate as a gift, to the king; 2. "gylden" alliterates with "gamelum."

The hilt was remarkable for other qualities than that it was of gold.

"Hrog[=a]r maelode, hylt sc[=e]awode, ealde l[=a]fe, on [=]m ws [=o]r writen fyrn-gewinnes, syan fl[=o]d ofsl[=o]h, gifen g[=e]otende, g[=i]ganta cyn; fr[=e]cne gef[=e]rdon; t ws fremde [=e]od [=e]cean Dryhtne; him s ende-l[=e]an urh wteres wylm Waldend sealde. Sw[=a] ws on [=]m scennum sc[=i]ran goldes urh r[=u]n-stafas rihte gemearcod, geseted ond gesd, hw[=a]m t sweord geworht, [=i]rena cyst, [=]rest w[=]re, wreoen-hilt ond wyrm-f[=a]h."[94]

"Hylt"[95] cannot mean the whole sword, since Hrothgar could look at only what was left of the sword. That was the "gylden hilt," which he held in his hand; and the expression "hylt sc[=e]awode" leaves no doubt that "gylden hilt" is not a designation of the whole sword. "Wreoen-hilt"[96] also obviously refers only to the hilt.

In no instance, therefore, in this connection, does the author of *Beowulf* use "hilt" to designate the whole sword; consequently, to write "gylden hilt" as one word and capitalize it is both arbitrary and illogical. There is, in fact, nothing in the poem to indicate that the sword had a name.

Furthermore, the author refers to other swords that were distinguished by being ornamented with gold. When Beowulf left the land of the Danes, it is said,

"H[=e] [=]m b[=a]t-wearde bunden golde
swurd gesealde."[97]

And when Beowulf returned to the land of the Geats and presented to Hygelac and Hygd the gifts he had received from Hrothgar,

"H[=e]t [=a] eorla hl[=e]o in gefetian, heao-r[=o]f cyning, Hr[=e]les l[=a]fe golde gegyrede; ns mid G[=e]atum [=a] sinc-m[=a]um s[=e]lra on sweordes h[=a]d; t h[=e] on B[=i]owulfes bearm [=a]legde."[98]

It is not said that either of these swords had a golden hilt; but it is plain that it was not unusual to represent a sword that possessed excellent qualities as being ornamented with gold, and the hilt is the part of the sword that naturally lends itself to ornamentation. Other examples of richly ornamented swords are King Arthur's sword, Excalibur, whose "pommel and haft were all of precious stones";[99] Roland's sword, Durendal, which had a golden hilt;[100] and the sword of Frothi II, which also had a golden hilt.[101]

The fact, therefore, that, both in regard to the giant-sword in *Beowulf* and King Hrolf's sword in the saga, the hilt is said to be golden proves nothing as to the identity of these two swords.

And when, both in the term "gylden hilt" and in the word "Gullinhjalti," the hilt of the sword is made prominent, it is due, in the one instance, to the fact that nothing but the hilt remains; in the other, to the fact that the word "hjalti" is just the word that the author must have in order to explain the origin of Hjalti's name.

A little more ought to be said about the propping-up of the dragon. That it served an excellent purpose is evident. It provided the occasion for Hjalti's asking for the king's sword, in the use of which he displayed his courage and from which he received his new name. Furthermore, Bjarki's interest in having Hott attack the beast and display his courage indicated that he knew that the beast was dead and that he had a special interest in having Hott recognized as a brave man. This, again, indicated that Bjarki had himself killed the beast and been the cause of the change in Hott's nature, for both of which he receives due credit. But it may be asked, when Bjarki propped the dead beast up, how could he know that events would take the turn they did? He could not know it. He relied on his resourcefulness to handle the situation, a resourcefulness on which he had drawn with success before. He was on hand in the morning to take note of developments, and we can imagine several possibilities that he might have had in mind. Had the king proposed that no risk should be taken with the beast, Bjarki could have requested and secured permission to attack it, taking Hott with him. Had the king himself proposed to attack the beast, or had he proposed that his warriors should attack it in a body, Bjarki could have said, "No, the king must not expose himself," or, "The king must not expose so many of his men at once; let me go." To which the king could have assented, whereupon Bjarki could have taken Hott with him and let Hott, at the last, proceed against the beast alone and knock it over. One can imagine other possibilities, which it is not necessary to enumerate here. To be sure, none of them would be so fortunate as the one represented as having occurred; but they would have enabled Hott to gain the reputation of being a brave man, and that is all Bjarki contemplated. That all turned out more fortunately than Bjarki had foreseen or even intended, enhances the interest of the story and illustrates the skill of the narrator, who chose to represent, as he had a right to do, that particular possibility as having actually occurred that produced the most satisfactory results. That Bjarki had no thought of credit for himself, redounds, in the estimation of the reader all the more to his credit; and it is a fitting reward that he gets full credit for all that he has done.

It seems, then, that Bjarki intended to deceive the king. He undoubtedly did; but the deception was not intended to mislead the king. Hott *was* brave and strong, and Bjarki knew it; and even if Hott's strength and bravery should gain recognition through the employment of a ruse that involved no real test, no harm would be done. The author, however, planned that all should turn out otherwise. The reader will also remember the deception practiced by the shepherd boy in the story from Jn Arnason's collection.[102] The boy, who is there the hero of the story, as is Bjarki in the *Hrlfssaga*, is represented as deceiving his master, but likewise without doing him appreciable harm, and furthermore without raising reflections on the part of the author as to the rectitude of his conduct.

Panzer says that Hott's explanation that the repeated breaking-in of the monster is due to the fact that the king's best men do not return home at that time of the year is a strange explanation.[103] But in regard to Hott's statement a distinction must be made between fact and opinion. It is a fact, as the saga immediately afterwards shows, that the king's berserks are not at home; but it is only Hott's opinion that, if they were at home, they would be able to put an end to the depredations of the monster. It was quite natural, however, that he should think so; for to such an abject coward as he was, it must have seemed that nothing could resist such warriors as these berserks were. That they were not at home was due to the fact that they were on one of their regular expeditions. But why they had not been retained at home to cope with the dragon is not explained. The first time it appeared, it came entirely unexpected. The next year there may have been a question as to whether it would appear or not. The third year it was definitely expected. It seems, therefore, that preparations would have been made to resist it; and when the berserks are not retained at home to cope with the monster, it is due to the exigencies of the story. The berserks might have been retained at home to cope unsuccessfully with the monster, or avoid coping with it at all as the king's other men did, and thus place Bjarki's feat of slaying it in the strongest relief. But by letting the berserks be absent at Christmas and return later, the author accomplished more than this. Bjarki slew the monster, which, in any treatment of the story, he must be represented as doing. He seized one of the berserks, who demanded that Bjarki recognize him as his superior as a warrior, and threw him down with great violence. This was a more spectacular method of showing superiority to the berserks than merely doing what they dared not attempt to do, or could not do. But it is especially in the treatment of Hott, that skillful manipulation of the story is displayed in having the berserks return home and resume their boastful manner, after Hott has become strong and daring. Compared with the king's best warriors it is still a question as to how strong and brave Hott now is. The question is answered when he is requested to admit his inferiority to the berserks; for he seizes the one who confronts him and treats him as Bjarki is treating one of the others. Thus, in the presence of King Hrolf and the court, Hott displays his superiority to the doughtiest of the king's famous warriors. Finally, poetic justice is also achieved, for the very men who had made fun of Hott and thrown bones at him are now compelled to recognize that he is the master of them all.

Panzer sees a deeper meaning, than evidently is intended, in the statement that, as Bjarki was about to attack the dragon, his sword stuck fast in the scabbard.[104] There is no reason, however, for regarding it as anything more than a melodramatic incident characteristic of medieval romances. It reminds one of the following statement by Wilbur L. Cross, which, with the omission of the reference to "giants" and "Merlin," characterizes the *Hrlfssaga* quite accurately and shows how it harmonizes with the spirit of medieval literature of its kind, "It is true that they [i.e., the Arthurian romances] sought to interest, and did interest, by a free employment of the marvellous, fierce encounters of knights, fights with giants and dragons, swords that would not out of their scabbards, and the enchantments of Merlin".[105]

The Stories in the BJARKARMUR *of Bjarki's Slaying the Wolf and Hjalti's Slaying the Bear.*

But what is the relation of this story to the corresponding stories in the *Bjarkarmur*? The stories in the *rmur* are as follows:—

"Flestir [o.]muu Hetti heldr, hann var ekki mli sneldr, einn dag fru eir t af h[o.]ll, sv ekki vissi hirin [o.]ll.
Hjalti talar er felmtinn fr, 'f[o.]rum vi ekki skgi nr, hr er s ylgr sem etr upp menn, okkr drepr hn ba senn.'

Ylgrin hljp r einum runn,
gurlig me gapanda munn,
h[o.]rmuligt var Hjalta vir,
honum skalf bi leggr og lir.

tpt Bjarki a henni gengr, ekki dvelr hann vi a lengr, h[o.]ggur sv a hamri std, hljp r henni ferligt bl.
'Kjstu Hjalti um kosti tv, kappinn B[o.]var talai sv, drekk n bl ea drep eg ig hr, dugrinn lz mr engi r.'
Ansar Hjalti af rnum m, 'ekki ori eg a drekka bl, ntir flest ef nauigr skal, n er ekki betra val.'
Hjalti gj[o.]rir sem B[o.]var bir, a bli fr eg hann lagist nir, drekkur san drykki rj, duga mun honum vi einn a rj.
Hugrinn x en miklast mttr, minst var honum litlu drttr, raunmj[o.]g sterkr og ramr sem tr[o.]ll, rifnuu af honum klin [o.]ll.
Sv er hann orinn harr i hug, hann hrist ekki jrna flug, burtu er n bleyinafn, B[o.]vari var hann a hreysti jafn." (IV, 58-66).

“Hann hefr fengi hjarta snjalt
af h[o.]rum mi,
fekk hann huginn og afli alt
af ylgjar bli.

grindur vandist grbj[o.]rn einn
garinn Hleiar,
var s margur vargrinn beinn
og va sveiar.

Bjarka er kent, a hjararhunda
hafi harm drepna,
ekki er hnum allvel hent
vi ta kepna.

Hrlfur bst og hir hans [o.]ll
a hna stri,
s skal mestr minni h[o.]ll
er mtir dri.

Beljandi hljp bj[o.]rninn framm
r bli krukku,
veifar snum vnda hramm,
sv virar hrukku.

Hjalti sr og horfir ,
er hafin er rma,
hafi hann ekki h[o.]ndum
nema hnefana tma.

Hrlfur fleygi a Hjalta
eim hildar vendi,
kappinn mti krummu br
og klti hendi.

Lagi hann san bj[o.]rninn brtt
vi bginn hgra,
bessi fell brar tt
og bar sig lgra.

Vann hann a til frga fyst
og fleira sar,
hans var lundin l[o.]ngum byst
leiki grar.

Hr me fekk hann Hjalta nafn
  hins hjartapra,
Bjarki var eigi betri en jafn
  vi bti skra." (V, 4-13).[106]

These stories seem, indeed, at first sight more rational than the story in the saga, and have features more in harmony with the account in Saxo; but this does not prove that they are earlier than the version in the saga. In the first place, by introducing two animals, where the other versions have only one, the author of the *rmur* has broken the unity of the story, a feature in which the story in the *Hrlfssaga* remains intact and as a consequence is nearer to the primitive form of the story as we find it in Saxo. In the second place, the author of the *rmur* made precisely the changes that were necessary to remove the most irrational features of the story as we find it in the *Hrlfssaga*. The troll-dragon, which is an unusual creature, has been supplanted by the more conventional creatures, a wolf and a bear; and by the employment of two animals, the necessity of causing a dead animal to be propped up and be apparently killed again, is avoided. Consistency in the treatment of Bjarki as the descendant of a bear is also observed to the extent that he is said to kill a wolf, not a bear; but this consistency has begun to fade and suffer to the extent that Bjarki accompanies Hrolf on a bear hunt. It is probable, however, that consistency in the treatment of Bjarki in this respect is not contemplated, but that when he is said to kill a wolf it is only that the larger and more dangerous animal may be reserved as the one on which Hjalti is to show his strength and courage and in order that an animal worthy of the king's attention may be reserved for the royal hunt. To eat wolf meat in order to gain strength has just as good warrant in Old Norse literature as to drink the blood of a bear;[107] this, in so far, justifies the introduction in the *rmur* of the wolf. But when Hjalti is made to *drink the blood* of the wolf, it seems to be another instance of the author's keeping in mind the version of the story in the *Hrlfssaga*, where Hjalti drinks the blood of the dragon. It is not necessary to go to Saxo's version for this.

It is said in the *rmur*, "One day they (Bjarki and Hjalti) went out of the hall, so that the king's men did not know of it." Why did they go out of the hall so that the king's men did not know of it? No reason is assigned; the deed is unmotivated. It seems to be a mere harking back to the statement in the *Hrlfssaga*,[108] that the two men left the hall secretly. But in the saga there is a reason for their leaving the hall secretly; the king has forbidden his men to leave the hall and expose themselves to attack. That, in the *rmur*, the men are said to leave the hall in the daytime, instead of at night, is a consequence of the substitution of the wolf for the troll-dragon; a wolf is usually hunted in the daytime. It might be surmised that their going out secretly is in imitation of the story as Saxo knew it. But this is not the case; Saxo does not say that Bjarki and Hjalti went out secretly.[109] The weakness of this feature of the story in the *rmur* has been observed by Panzer, who believes, nevertheless, that the *rmur* represent an earlier form of the story than the one in the saga. He says, "Zweifeln mchte man nur, ob das Motiv des heimlichen Auszugs der beiden nicht in den *Rmur* flschlich in den ersten Kampf gesetzt ist, wo es ganz unbegrndet steht, statt in den zweiten, wo es allein motiviert erscheint."[110] But this is not the correct explanation. The author of the *rmur* for some reason, such as a wish to rationalize the story, but which, however, we can only surmise, decided to make radical changes in it. In the first instance he substitutes a wolf for the dragon, but otherwise, considering the material he is going to use in the story of the fight with the bear, retains as much as he can of the story as it is in the saga. Thus the idea of Bjarki's and Hjalti's going out secretly is retained, but without motivation; and if we did not have the story in the saga for comparison, perhaps this deficiency would not have been noticed. Even as it is, Panzer is the only one who has called attention to it.

Referring to the story as Saxo has it, Mllenhoff,[111] ten Brink,[112] Olrik,[113] and Deutschbein[114] speak of Bjarki's going on a hunt. This is hardly correct and requires a little attention, for, if, in Saxo's version, Bjarki went on a hunt, the account given by Saxo is nearer to the first story in the *rmur* than if he did not. But Saxo does not say that Bjarki went on a hunt. He says: "Talibus operum meritis exultanti nouam de se siluestris fera uictoriam prebuit. Vrsum quippe eximie magnitudinis obuium sibi inter dumeta factum iaculo confecit, comitemque suum Ialtonem, quo uiribus maior euaderet, applicato ore egestum belue cruorem haurire iussit. Creditum namque erat, hoc pocionis genere corporei roboris incrementa prestari."[115] The circumstances immediately preceding the slaying of the bear were such, that it is highly improbable that, at that particular time, he would go on a hunt. It will be remembered that there was to be a wedding in the royal residence; that Agnar was to marry the king's sister; that Agnar took offense at Bjarki's manner of defending Hjalti, whereupon a fight ensued and Bjarki killed Agnar and his warriors. But if Bjarki did not go on a hunt for the bear, how did he come to meet it, and in a thicket at that? The lack of more details, the lack of motivation for going on a hunt in the midst of, or immediately following, the stirring events just mentioned, and utter lack of connection with what precedes, show that Saxo, who, with this story, begins to set the stage, so to speak, for the last grand act of King Hrolf's life, concluded to insert it at this juncture as the most appropriate and effective place he had for it, and then, to add a touch of realism and supply a retreat where the bear would be unobserved by the men, and unwarned of their approach, until they were close upon it, said that Bjarki met it in a thicket. The idea of supplying a motive and observing such consistency as we find in connection with the corresponding story in the *Hrlfssaga* never occurred to him. The author of the *rmur* may have known of the version of the story familiar to Saxo, though it is not probable; but the point here is, that he is not following this version when he represents Bjarki as having slain an animal for which he has presumably (though the *rmur* do not make the matter clear) gone on a hunt.

The author was under no more obligation than Saxo was, to say that Bjarki and Hjalti went out secretly, and the idea is not contained in Saxo's account. But the author of the *rmur*, observing what pains the author of the saga took to motivate the going out secretly, felt that this feature of the story was so important that it must be retained, and so he retained it without motivation.

In Saxo, Hjalti shows no fear when the bear is met, and he does not refuse to drink the animal's blood. But in the *rmur* there is the same kind of fear as in the saga. In the saga, however, the author has found an excellent setting for Hjalti's fear; it is beyond improvement; while the ferocity of the man-eating wolf, in the *rmur*, is stretched to the utmost limit, in order to preserve the spirit of the heroic. Furthermore, when Hjalti had drunk of the blood of the wolf, he had courage "enough for fighting with one man." How did the author know that he had just courage "enough for fighting with one man"? According to the next statement, namely "his courage increased, his strength waxed, he became very strong, mighty as a troll, all his clothes burst open," he seemed, in fact, to have gained strength enough for fighting with several men. Again, "he was equal to Bothvar in courage." How did the author know it? He knew it from the version of the story in the saga, where it is said that Hjalti had wrestled long with Bothvar, and, thus having tried his strength on Bothvar, told him, "nor shall I be afraid of you henceforth." The saga does not say that Hjalti had courage "enough for fighting with one man" or "he was equal to Bothvar in courage." These statements are deductions that the author of the *rmur* made from the story in the saga, in the light of subsequent events.

In the *rmur*, it is said that Hjalti "became very strong, mighty as a troll, all his clothes burst open." Why, or whence, this reference to a troll? Another harking back to the *Hrlfssaga,* another deduction made from the story in the saga. The saga does not say that Hott acquired any of the characteristics of a troll. He is given the desired strength without any reference to the strength of a troll. But when the *rmur* say that he became "mighty as a troll," it amounts to saying, "Hjalti is no longer represented as having drunk the blood of a troll and eaten some of its heart, as is the case in the *Hrlfssaga*, but let it be understood, nevertheless, that the strength he has acquired is no less than that of a troll." The troll-dragon has been eliminated, but so great, in the *rmur*, has the strength of Hjalti become that it now equals that of the very monster, the troll, which, in the saga, he feared to such an extent that it rendered him pitiable in the extreme. Here again the author of the *rmur* inserted an element that is wholly foreign to his story and unsuggested by it, but that is suggested by the saga, and that he probably never would have thought of, had he not known of the version of the story that is contained in the saga.

Furthermore, the *rmur* say, "The folds at Hleidargard were attacked by a gray bear; many such beasts were there far and wide thereabout. Bjarki was told that it had killed the herdsmen's dogs; it was not much used to contending with men." This is still another harking back to the *Hrlfssaga*, and confirms what has been said on pp. 29 ff., that the monster in the saga is a cattle-attacking monster, not a hall-attacking monster. "The folds were attacked," "it had killed the herdsmen's dogs," "it was not much used to contending with men."

The fact that dogs are here said to be killed, but not in the saga, need hardly be mentioned. The idea of dogs is easily associated with that of cattle, especially when, as here, the dogs are "herdsmen's dogs."

Again, we notice the statement in the *rmur* that "Hrolf tossed to Hjalti his sword." Has he been informed since the slaying of the wolf, that Hjalti is now a courageous man? Perhaps; but nothing is said about it in the *rmur*. Since Bjarki took pains to go on the wolf hunt secretly, and since we are not informed that what occurred on that hunt has become known or that it has become known that Hjalti is now a courageous man, the presumption is that the king does not know it, and we are surprised at his unmotivated action in treating Hjalti in this unexpected manner. And if Hjalti is now known to be such a hero that Hrolf feels warranted in placing reliance on him to the extent that he tosses him his sword at this critical juncture, why has Hjalti taken part in the hunt with "nothing in his hands"? In the saga it is not said that Hjalti has nothing in his hands; his motive in asking for the king's sword has no connection with whether he has anything in his hands or not.[116] But the author of the *rmur*, having apparently missed the point in the saga, assumes that, when Hjalti asks for the king's sword, it is because he has no weapon of his own. Hence, without realizing, apparently, the anomalous situation in which he places Hjalti, who is now strong and courageous, he represents him as taking part in the bear hunt empty-handed, though there is no indication that Hjalti thinks that he can cope with the animal without a weapon.

In the *Hrlfssaga*, it is said that Bjarki killed a dragon by plunging his sword under its shoulder. In the *rmur*, it is said that Hjalti killed a bear by plunging his sword into its right shoulder. This is another harking back to the *Hrlfssaga*. Hjalti has now become as courageous as Bjarki; he kills a live animal (instead of knocking over a dead one), and he kills it in just the same way that Bjarki killed the dragon. It can not be assumed that the author of the *rmur* and the author of the saga employed this manner of dispatching the animal without any knowledge on the part of the one as to what was contained in the account of the other. In fact, it is taken for granted by all writers on the subject that the later account is an altered version of the earlier account. Hence, either this episode in the *rmur* is modeled after that in the saga, and Hjalti is made to kill the bear in the same way that Bjarki killed the dragon, or the episode in the saga is modeled after that in the *rmur*, and Bjarki is made to kill the dragon in the same way that Hjalti killed the bear. Is there any doubt as to what has occurred? The former is natural and to be expected, and is probably what has taken place, because: 1. in all the versions of the story Hjalti is represented as having undergone a change that has caused him to become very much like Bjarki—"equal to Bjarki," as it is stated in the *rmur*, where he is represented as having killed a ferocious beast in the same manner that Bjarki, in the saga, killed a winged monster; 2. it was not unusual to represent dragons as having been killed by being pierced under the shoulder,[117] since a dragon had to be pierced where its scales did not prevent the entrance of a weapon into its body; 3. since there is no special reason why a bear, which is vulnerable in all parts of the body, should be represented as being pierced through the shoulder, the manner in which Hjalti is said to have killed the bear is evidently another unmotivated incident in the *rmur* that is imitated from a motivated incident in the saga.

What the author of the *rmur* has done to give the story the form in which we find it in his composition is quite plain. He noticed that, as the monster in the saga attacked the folds at Hleidargard, the situation was very much like that at the beginning of the story about Bothvar in the saga, where a bear is said to have attacked the cattle of King Hring, Bothvar's father.[118] But a bear is a real, not an imaginary, animal, and King Hring took a creditable part in the effort to dispatch it. Hence, this story was substituted for the story about the troll-dragon and adapted to the circumstances,

King Hrolf himself taking the lead in the hunt and thus acting in a manner that seemed more to his credit than the way he acted in regard to the monster in the saga.

This story, namely that the man whose cattle have been killed by a bear goes with his men and hunts it down and kills it, is the same that we have in connection with the early life both of Ulf and of Bjarki, where the bear is represented as being the great-grandfather of the former, but the father of the latter. The bear-ancestor feature was not applicable in the connection in which the story is used in the *rmur*; hence, it was omitted. Now, did this story spring up spontaneously and independently in all these three instances? No, Bjarki and Ulf got their reputed ancestry from the Siward story; and this bear hunt story they got from a common source through contact with each other, or Bjarki got it from Ulf. The author of the *rmur*, liking it better than the last part of the dragon story in the saga, as most modern readers also have done, took it from the version contained in the saga of the early life of Bjarki and used it for letting Hjalti display his courage. As a result, he modified the story where it applies to the early life of Bjarki. He has two sets of three sons each, while the saga has only one set; and, what is still more suspicious, there is a Bothvar in each set. This is the same kind of separation or repetition as the *rmur* later make with regard to the dragon story, dividing it into a wolf story and a bear story. Again, as Finnur Jnsson, summarizing the account in the *rmur* of the death of Bjarki's father, says, "Bjrn forflges, flygter ud i et skr og drbes der af jarlens mnd p et skib (en strk afvigelse fra sagaen)."[119] This divergence was plainly introduced to make the story different from the story that, in substance, was replaced and that was transferred to where Hjalti displays his courage. In the saga, Bjarki's mother is called Bera (she-bear),[120] not Hildr, as in the *rmur*; and that the name Bera is the earlier of the two there can be no doubt.

Furthermore, we find in the *rmur* another of the characteristic traces that the author left when he tampered with the dragon story. In the saga, in connection with Bjarki's early life, it is said that when the bear was hunted, it killed all the dogs, but was itself soon after killed by the men. From this the author concluded that it was death on dogs, but could not contend successfully with men. Hence, he says, "Bjarki was told that it had killed the herdsmen's dogs;[121] it was not much used to contending with men." This statement must, therefore, mean, if it means anything, that the bear was not really dangerous to men or, at any rate, not as dangerous as one would naturally suppose. Hjalti must have known this as well as Bjarki, for it was probably he who gave Bjarki the information about the beast, as he did in the corresponding situation in the saga and in the story of the slaying of the wolf. If this was the case, the bravery that Hjalti displays in attacking the animal suffers considerably. The statement reminds us of the situation in the *Hrlfssaga*. Just as Hjalti knocked over a dragon that was not dangerous because it was dead, so, in the *rmur*, he dispatched a bear that was not particularly dangerous because "it was not much used to contending with men." In the former instance, however, the feat was not the real test of his courage; in the latter instance, it was.

In the saga, Bjarki knew that the dragon was harmless, because he had killed it; and his knowledge of its harmlessness is vital to the latter part of the dragon story. In the *rmur*, he is informed that the bear is not so dangerous as one would suppose. But his knowledge of this circumstance has no bearing on the story whatever; everything would have proceeded just as it did if he had been without this information. But in spite of the fact that the bear "was not much used to contending with men," "the men fled" when it "ran from its lair and shook its baleful paws." The author is evidently trying to ride two steeds going in different directions. On the one hand, he has in mind the story of the bear with which Bjarki's father was identified and which was killed by the king's men, and the story of the dead propped-up dragon, which was, of course, not dangerous; on the other hand, he wishes to represent Hjalti's feat of killing the bear, which, in the *rmur*, the king's men avoided, as, in the saga, they avoided the dragon, as a notable achievement.

Finally, "Hrolf and all his men" took part in the hunt; but, as already stated, when the bear appeared, "the men fled." The statement, "the men fled;" introduces a feature that is wanting in the account in the *Hrlfssaga* of how Bjarki's father, who had been transformed into a bear by his stepmother, was hunted down and killed. It reminds us of the situation in the saga where King Hrolf and his men avoid the winged monster by remaining indoors when it is expected. In the saga, Bjarki, of course, did not avoid the monster; but whether, in the *rmur*, the king fled is uncertain. He was, in any event, near enough to Hjalti to toss Hjalti his sword. Bjarki, however, must have fled; and while that would be strange under any circumstances, it would be particularly strange in the present instance, since he knew that the bear "was not much used to contending with men."

Considering the dragon story in the saga and the corresponding stories in the *rmur*, it is apparent that there is no comparison between them as regards skill in composition; and that, while the stories in the *rmur* throw no light on the story in the saga, the full significance of the *rmur* stories appears only when they are read in the light of the story in the saga. Therefore, when Finnur Jnsson says, "Sprger vi om, hvad der er oprindeligst, er der i og for sig nppe tvivl om, at rimerne her har af t dyr gjort to (ulvinden og grbjrnen), s at sagaen p dette punkt m antages at have bedre bevaret det gte," he is undoubtedly right; but when he continues, "Dette bestyrkes kraftig ved, at dette hallen hjemsgende uhyre intet andet er end et om end ndret og afbleget minde om Grendel i *Bjovulf*,"[122] he is, as the evidence also shows, undoubtedly wrong.

The fact of the matter is that the account in the *rmur* of the killing of the bear, though brief, is so confused and indefinite that it does not bear analysis; and this is further evidence of the fact that the author of the *rmur* clumsily re-worked material that he found in the *Hrlfssaga* version of Bjarki's career, and for the dragon story, which is a good story, substituted two poor ones, namely the wolf story and the bear story.

But the troll-dragon having been eliminated and the bear story selected as the one to be used in connection with Hjalti's display of his newly acquired bravery, for which purpose it is, indeed, on account of the presence of the king and his court, more appropriate than for giving Hjalti an opportunity to imbibe secretly an animal's blood, another story had to be devised to account for Hjalti's strength and courage. The wolf was the next fiercest animal available that the author could think of. He therefore invented a wolf story and placed it first; and, as the examination of it has shown,[123] a late and very poor invention it was, bearing manifest traces of the influence of the dragon story in the saga.

Conclusion.

The principal results attained in the foregoing consideration of the dragon story in the *Hrlfssaga* and the corresponding stories in the *Bjarkarmur* may be stated briefly as follows:—

1. The story in Saxo is the earliest story we have of the slaying of an animal by Bjarki in order that Hjalti may drink its blood and acquire strength and courage.

2. Bjarki having acquired a reputed bear-ancestry from the fictitious story about Siward, the saga consistently takes this into account and substitutes a dragon, also acquired from the story about Siward, for the bear, which, in Saxo's version, is the kind of animal that Bjarki slays.

3. To motivate Bjarki's going forth secretly to slay the monster at night, a well defined type of Christmas-troll story is employed and the dragon is given the nature of a troll that comes on Christmas Eve and attacks the cattle of the king, who, on account of the terrible nature of the monster, commands his men to stay in the house the night it is expected.

4. That Bjarki may be given credit a) for slaying the monster and b) for making a brave man of the coward Hott, and that c) Hott's change of nature may become apparent and d) a suitable opportunity and plausible reason may be devised for changing his name to Hjalti, the dead dragon is propped up and, in connection with the discovery of the ruse, the story is manipulated so that the saga-man realizes his fourfold purpose.

5. It is highly improbable that the sword-name "Gullinhjalti" in the saga is connected with the words "gylden hilt" in *Beowulf.* The use of the word "Gullinhjalti" in the saga is not arbitrary or artificial, but a logical result of the situation; and, as the discussion of the matter has shown, the attempt to identify Gullinhjalti with the giant-sword in *Beowulf* is based on a mere superficial similarity, in which a substantial foundation is altogether lacking.

6. The *Bjarkarmur* are a later composition than the *Hrlfssaga.*[124] The author of the *rmur* has discarded the story of the troll-dragon, has substituted for it the story of the bear hunt connected with the account of Bjarki's early life, has invented a new story about Bjarki's early life, and has invented the story about the wolf hunt to give an opportunity for the introduction of the blood-drinking episode. In the stories of the wolf hunt and the bear hunt, the *rmur* contain several unmotivated statements that are plainly based on the story as we have it in the saga; and, on the whole, the two stories in the *rmur* represent such decidedly poor workmanship in the art of

narration that recourse must be had to the story in the saga for a realization of the significance of some of the incidents contained in the *rmur*. The *rmur* must therefore be left entirely out of account in any attempt to identify Bjarki with Beowulf, or in attempting to connect Bjarki's deeds with those of other heroes, as, for instance, that of Hereward in *Gesta Herwardi*.[125]

In regard to some particulars, these conclusions differ from the conclusions at which others have arrived; in regard to others, they agree with them. This, however, is a mere matter of chance; for, where some have affirmed and others have denied, it is impossible to avoid agreeing with one party or the other, whatever conclusion an investigation may lead to. Nor should there be any desire to strive for what is new, merely for its own sake. The merit of the foregoing discussion, if it has any, lies in the explanation of the story about Bjarki and the dragon in the *Hrlfssaga* and the explanation of the relation between this story and the corresponding stories in the *Bjarkarmur*. This explanation is new, and the writer believes that he has given sufficient reasons to prove that it is correct. If it is correct, it shows that the stories in the *rmur* are less admirable compositions than they are usually held to be; it shows that the dragon story in the saga is a better composition than it is usually taken to be; and, finally, it establishes the fact that the dragon story in the *Hrlfssaga* has no connection whatever with the Grendel story or the dragon story in *Beowulf*.[126]

II

FRATTR

The first appearance of Hroar (Hrothgar) in literature is in *Widsith* and *Beowulf*, where we become acquainted with him as the famous King of the Danes. Helgi (Halga) appears first in *Beowulf*, where he is scarcely more than mentioned. Hroar and Helgi belong to the most famous group of ancient kings in Denmark and appear repeatedly in old Scandinavian literature. The account of them in the *Frattr* which introduces the *Hrlfssaga*, is, briefly summarized, as follows.

Halfdan and Frothi were brothers, the sons of a king, and each was the ruler of a kingdom. Halfdan had two sons, Hroar and Helgi, and a daughter, Signy, the oldest of the three children, who was married to Earl Svil while her brothers were still young. The boys' foster-father was Regin. Near Halfdan's capital was a wooded island, on which lived an old man, Vifil, a friend of Halfdan. Vifil had two dogs, called Hopp and Ho, and was skilled in soothsaying.

Frothi, envying his brother the crown of Denmark, attacked his capital with a large army, reduced it to ashes, and took Halfdan captive and put him to death. Regin took his foster-sons, Hroar and Helgi, to the island and placed them in the care of Vifil, in order that they might not fall into the hands of Frothi. Vifil took them to a cave (earth-hut), where they usually stayed at night; but in the daytime they sported in the grove. Frothi made every effort to locate them and make away with them, calling in witches and wise men from all over the land to tell him where they were, but in vain. Then he called in soothsayers, who told him the boys were not on the mainland, nor far from the court. The king mentioned Vifil's island, and they told him to look for the boys there. Twice he sent men to search for them, but the men failed to find them. Then the king went himself. Vifil, who knew the king was coming, met him on the strand as if by chance, pretending to be looking after his sheep; and when the king bade his men seize Vifil, the old man said, "Do not detain me, or the wolves will destroy my sheep," and cried out, "Hopp and Ho, guard my sheep." The king asked him to whom he was calling; he said, to his dogs. But he had told the boys before, that, when he called out the names of his dogs, they should hide in the cave. The king failed to find the boys and returned; but Vifil told the boys that it was not safe for them to remain on the island and sent them to their brother-in-law, Svil, saying that they would some day be famous, unless, perchance, something prevented it.

Hroar was now twelve years old and Helgi ten. The boys returned to Svil, but, calling themselves Hrani and Hamur, did not tell him who they were; and as they always wore masks, their identity remained unknown to him.

Frothi invited Svil to a feast. Hroar and Helgi expressed a wish to join him; but Svil commanded them to remain at home. Nevertheless, when Svil and his retinue had started off, Helgi got an untamed colt, and mounting it with his face toward the horse's tail, set out, acting all the while very foolishly. Hroar also mounted a colt, and joined him; and the two overtook the company. They galloped back and forth beside Svil's retinue, until finally Helgi's mask fell off, and then Signy recognized him. She began to weep, and when Svil asked her the cause of her distress, she informed him of her discovery. Svil tried to get the boys to return home; but, though they now were on foot and remained in the rear, they persisted in accompanying him on his visit to Frothi.

When they arrived at Frothi's, Frothi began to hunt for the boys, and bade a witch, who had come to the hall, to try her skill in finding them. She told him that they were in the hall. Then Signy threw her a gold ring, and the witch said that what she had just stated was false. Frothi threatened to torture her if she did not tell the truth; and she said that unless he soon prevented it, which he would not do, the boys would be his death. But the boys, terrified, fled to the wood. The king ordered his men to seize them; but Regin put out the lights in the hall, and, in the confusion that followed, those who were friendly to the boys used the opportunity to obstruct those who would pursue them. Frothi vowed that he would take vengeance at a more suitable time on those who had assisted the boys, but added, "Let us now drink and feast"; and this they did till the men lay in a drunken stupor in a heap on the floor.

Regin rode out to where the boy's were, but would not return their salutation. In fact, he pretended to be angry. They wondered what this meant, and followed him. Helgi thought that Regin wanted to help them, but without violating his oath to the king. Then Regin said to himself, so that the boys heard it, "If I had a matter to settle with the king, I would burn this grove." They took the hint and started a fire. Svil came out with all his men and bade them aid the boys, and Regin took measures to get all his men and relatives out of the hall. The king awoke from a dream, in which the goddess of the nether world was summoning him. He discovered the fire, and learning who had set it, offered the boys peace on their own terms; but terms of peace were denied. Frothi then retired from the door of the hall, hoping to escape by an underground passage; but at the entrance stood Regin, who blocked his progress, and he returned into the hall and perished in the flames. His wife, Sigrith (now mentioned for the first time), the mother of Hroar and Helgi, refused to leave the hall and perished also.

The boys thanked their brother-in-law, Svil, and their foster-father, Regin, and all the others who had helped them, and gave the men rich gifts. The boys subdued the whole land and seized the late king's possessions; and for a while the time passed without the occurrence of anything worthy of special mention.

At this time there was a king by the name of Northri, who ruled over a part of England. Hroar often passed long intervals at the court of Northri, supporting him against his enemies and defending his land. Hroar married gn, the daughter of Northri, shared the royal power with his father-in-law, and after Northri's death succeeded to the throne of Northumberland. Helgi remained at home, and, by agreement with Hroar, became sole King of Denmark.

In Saxo's seventh book, there is another version of the same story. The features in which it chiefly varies from the version in the *Hrlfssaga* are as follows.

Halfdan's name has become Harald; Hroar's and Helgi's names have become Harald and Halfdan; Earl Svil has become Siward, King of Sweden; Signy has become a daughter of Karl, governor of Gautland, and wife of Harald (Frothi's brother). Envy and the quarrelsomeness of Frothi's wife and Harald's wife cause Frothi to engage men to murder Harald. Frothi tries to avoid suspicion of being the author of the crime, but in vain; the people believe he is guilty. When he seeks the boys of the murdered king, to put them out of the way, their foster-parents bind the claws of wolves under the boys' feet and let them run about and fill a neighboring morass and the snow-covered ground with their tracks, whereupon the children of bond-women are put to death and the children's bodies torn to pieces and strewn about. This is done to give the impression that the boys have been torn to pieces by wolves. Then the boys are concealed in a large hollow oak, where food is brought them under the pretence that they are dogs. Dogs' names are also applied to them. The episode with the witch is present, but other men and women with superhuman power are not introduced. The whereabouts of the boys begins to be bruited about, and Ragnar, their foster-father, flees with them to Fyen. He is captured and admits that he has the boys in his protection; but he begs the king not to injure them, calls attention to the foulness of doing them harm, and promises, in case they make any disturbance in the kingdom, to report the matter to the king. Frothi, whose severity Ragnar thus transforms into mildness, spares the boys, and for many years they live in security. When they are grown up, they go to Seeland. Their friends urge them to avenge their father's death, and this they promise to do. Ragnar, when he hears of this, reports it to the king in accordance with his promise, whereupon the king proceeds against them with an army. In desperation, the boys pretend insanity; and, as it is considered shameful to attack people who are insane, the king again spares them. But in the night the boys set fire to his hall, after having stoned the queen to death; and Frothi, having hid himself in a secret underground passage, perishes from the effects of smoke and gas. The boys share the crown, ruling the kingdom by turns.

Before proceeding further, it would be well to have a summary of the relations of the Danish kings concerned, up to the last stage of development, the stage with which we are dealing; and this summary is best supplied by quoting the following from Olrik's *Danmarks Heltedigtning:[127]*—

"Der er en fortlling, som bar banet Skjoldungsagnene vej til manges hjrter, i vort rhundrede ikke mindre end p selve sagafortllingens tid: sagnene om de to unge kongesnner Hroar og Helge, der m skjule sig for deres faders morder og tronraner, farbroderen Frode, men som efter en rkke ventyrlige oplevelser p den enlige holm og i selve kongsgrden ser lejlighed til at fuldfre hvnen og hve sig p, tronen. En strlende begyndelse p den navnkundige kongets mange skbner! Det er denne fortllings udspring, vi nu skal sge.

"Tidligst foreligger den i en norsk saga fra 12te rh., der bner Sakses 7de bog; men smukkest er den islandske *Hrlfssaga.* Desuden foreligger den kort og krnikeagtig i den islandske *Skj[o.]ldungasaga*, som lader brodermorderen hedde Ingjald og ikke Frode.

"Med disse kilder nr vi dog kun til det egenlige sagamands-omrde, Norge og Island. I Danmark er fortllingen ukendt; og Sakse og Svend gesn er enige on den lige modsatte overlevering: det er Halvdan, der slr sin broder Frode eller begge sine brdre ihjel for at vinde herredmmet alene. Det er ikke rimeligt, at den danske overlevering skulde have dels forvansket, dels tabt den mere gte norske; ti fortllingen om de forfulgte kongesnner er s let at huske som et ventyr og vil vanskelig g i glemme, naar den frst er hrt.

"Ogs den ldste sagnform, Beovulfkvadets, kender kampen om herredmmet imellem Halvdan og Frode; men der er den forskel, at den ene er konge over Danerne, den anden over Had-Barderne, og det er imellem disse to folkestammer, striden udkmpes. Det synes snarest, som om Frode er falden i kampen (flere forskere opfatter stedet sledes); i hvert fald tillader sammenhngen nppe, at Halvdan kan vre falden imod Frode. For s vidt str denne ldste form nrmest ved den senere danske overlevering, fjrnere fra den norske.

"Som Halvdans broderdrab fortlles hos Sakse og Svend gesn, str det lsrevet, vi kan godt sige meningslst. Det ver ingen episk indflydelse p, Skjoldungernes liv, og der rammer heller ikke Halvdan eller hans t nogen moralsk gengldelse. Med god grund undrer Sakse sig over denne livsskbne, at den grumme drabsmand kan d en fredelig dd i sin alderdom; ti det er ganske mod heltedigtningens nd. Forklaringen derp har vi til dels i den ldre sagnform: broderkampen er opstet af den gamle folkekamp, hvor Had-Barderne l, under for Danerne; men tillige m der vre bristet en episk sammenknytning. I nste slgtled af Skjoldungtten er det et ret gammelt sagnmotiv, at Hrrik overfalder og flder Hroar; ban har sikkert vret opfattet som Frodes sn og hvner, ikke blot i norsk men ogs i gammel dansk overlevering.

"Den srlig norske form er da bleven til, ved at man vendte broderdrabet om. Det er en sagndannelse af ganske samme art som den, der gjorde Hrrik til Hroars drabsmand; heltetten kom til at st skyldfri. Det nste trin var at udvikle denne ny situation med Halvdansnnernes fredlshed og deres faderhvn. Vi har en gammel kilde, der viser, at udviklingen virkelig er get i disse to trin. *Grottesangen* slutter med spdom on, at 'Yrsas sn [Rolf] skal hvne

Halvdans drab p, Frode.' Da kvadet synes digtet af en Nordmand i 10de rh., har vi i alt fire tidsfstede udviklingstrin af sagnet:

> "1. Danekongen Halvdan kmper med Hadbardekongen Frode og bar formodenlig fldet ham (*Beovulf*).
>
> "2. Skjoldungen Halvdan kmper med sin broder Frode on riget og flder ham (danske sagn).
>
> "3. Skjoldungen Frode drber (sin broder) Halvdan, snnesonnen Rolf hvner det (*Grottesangen*, 10de rh., norsk).
>
> "4. Skjoldungen Frode overfalder sin broder Halvdan og drber ham; snnerne Hroar og Helge redder livet og hvner siden deres faders dd (norsk og islandsk saga, 12te, 13de, 14de rh.).
>
> "Iflge dette m sagaen om Helges og Hroars barndom vre opstet mellem r 1000 (950) og r 1100, snarest nr ved den frste tid.[128]

"Langt vigtigere end tidspunktet er dog *arten af denne omdannelse*. Vi str her foran det strste skel, der forekommer i heltedigtningens levnedslb: overgangen fra den lse skare af smsagn, der slutter sig forklarende og udfyldende omkring kvadene, til *sagaen*, der selvstndig og i lbende sammenhng gr rede for heltenes liv. Netop ved Skjoldungsagnene mtte denne overgang blive afgrende. Nr Halvdans mord var det frste punkt i slgtens historie, kunde man umulig unddrage sig fra klart og alsidig at belyse dets flger. Det var selvflgeligt, at Frode ogs strbte at rydde Halvdans to snner af vejen; sledes fremkom sagnene om fosterfdre og venner, der sgte at skjule dem. For Helge og Hroar mtte den eneste vej til deres fdrene trone g gennem kamp; deraf opstod da sagnet on hvn over Frode.

"Enkeite trk i denne digtning bar sagamanden natrligvis hentet fra den overleverede rigdom af sagn. Det er allerede forlngst indset, at vsenlige trk skyldes ln fra sagnet on *Amled*, den unge kongesn, der redder sit liv ved foregivet vanvid, da hans farbroder bar hvet sig p tronen ved mord p hans fader."

The chapter from which the above is taken contains about a page more. Olrik says, "Sagnet om Helge og Hroar er dog som helhed noget ganske andet end den specielle Amledtype." He refers by way of comparison to the life of Sigurd the Volsung, to the myth of Romulus and Remus, and the corresponding myth of the Greek twins of Thebes, Thessaly, and Arcadia; and concludes thus: "Er der fremmed indflydelse ved dens fdsel [i.e., the story of Hroar's and Helgi's childhood], m den vre svag og let strejfende. Snarere m man opfatte sagnet sledes, at dette mne har en livskraft til stadig at fdes p ny, hver gang den unge belt vokser op efter faderens drab. Motivet er s nrliggende, s ubetinget heltegyldigt, at da Skjoldungsagaerne voksede frem p folkemunde, mtte de bnes med denne digtning; den var stadig—s at sige—lige ndvendig for at stemple den store helteskikkelse."

The story about the Scylding kings in its various phases (except the first, in *Beowulf*) is found in Denmark and in the Old Norse. Among the Danes and Norwegians (including Icelanders), therefore, we must look for an explanation of this last stage of development. But in the north of England were many Danes and Norwegians, and, as has already been pointed out, the story about Bothvar Bjarki was known in England and acquired distinct features there.[129] To England, then, we turn for an explanation of the main features of the Hroar-Helgi story.

Furthermore, the story is due to a combination of influences. Evidence of this is the fact that it shows unmistakable influence of the Hamlet story, which, however, does not furnish an explanation of the story as a whole. And the fact that the story about Hroar and Helgi was not a native product of England and had no roots in the soil of the country, so to speak, which tended to hold it within bounds, but was an imported story circulating rather loosely, far from the scene of the supposed events related, would make it peculiarly susceptible to extraneous influences adapted to aid in its development.

The first influence to which the Hroar-Helgi story was subjected was plainly the "exile-return" type of story, whose general characteristics are stated by Deutschbein as follows:—

"Das Reich eines Knigs, der nur einen jungen unerwachsenen Sohn hat, wird eines Tages vom Feinde berfallen. Der Vater fllt im blutigen Kampfe. Die Rettung des jungen Thronerben ist mit Schwierigkeiten verbunden—hufig steht dem jungen Frstensohn in der ussersten Not ein getreuer Eckhart zur Seite, eine feststehende Figur in unserm Typus. Der Knigssohn wird in Sicherheit gebracht, in der Fremde zunchst in niedriger Stellung, meist unter angenommenem Namen, wchst er zu einem tchtigen Recken heran, bis zuletzt die Zeit der Heimkehr gekommen ist. Er nimmt furchtbare Rache an den Mrdern seines Vaters und gewinnt sein Erbe zurck; wesentliche Dienste leistet ihm dabei ein oder mehrere treue Anhnger seines Vaters, die in der Heimat zurckgeblieben sind.

"Eine Abart dieses Typus weist einen anderen Eingang auf: statt usserer Feinde sind es nahe Verwandte (Oheim, Stiefvater, Stiefbrder), die den jungen Prinzen seines Vaters berauben und ihm selbst nachstellen. Diese Form bezeichnen wir mit B, die Hauptform mit A."[130]

The Hroar-Helgi story has two young princes; otherwise, it conforms exactly to type B.

Frothi, Halfdan's brother (*Hrlfssaga* version), attacks him with an army and defeats and slays him. The boys are taken by Regin, their foster-father, to a neighboring island for safety (this, however, is being sent abroad with a limited application of the term), where they live with a shepherd in a cave, responding, when necessary, to the names of dogs. There they remain until they are twelve and ten years old respectively, when they return to their sister and brother-in-law, who, together with Regin, render the boys valuable assistance. They take frightful vengeance on their father's slayer by setting fire to his hall and forcing him to perish in the flames.

The third stage having been reached in the development of the Hroar-Helgi story, in which the brother who is slain is avenged by one of his descendants, it was easy and natural for it to fall in with the "exile-return" type. The type is not an artificial type, it is founded on human nature. The guileless and weak must yield to the designing and strong. History teems with illustrations of the fact that he wears the crown who can win it and hold it. Where a kingdom is the prize, a man is under a mighty temptation when he sees that he can seize it by brushing aside a weak ruler and a still weaker heir, or, the ruler being out of the way, the young heir only. And it is natural that, the young heir surviving, he should avenge a murdered parent, regain the crown, and not permit the usurper to enjoy the fruits of his crime unmolested. Friends each party would also have, actuated, if by nothing else, by self-interest, which is bound up in the success of their chief. What the Hroar-Helgi story in its third stage of development may have been we do not know. We are only told that "Yrsa's son will avenge Frothi's murder of Halfdan." But the story was well prepared for the type it was to assume.

That the story was clearly regarded as one of this type is evident from the fact that in Johannes Bramis' *Historia Regis Waldei* Frodas is the usurper of the throne which by right belongs to Waldef.[131] It is not necessary to repeat the story; it has all the characteristics of the "exile-return" type. As a whole, it has no connection with the Hroar-Helgi story; and it contains the only instance known of the use of Frothi outside the story where he originally belongs. But he is so typically the same person, with the same unlovable characteristics, that he can be none other than the Frothi who plays such a conspicuous part in the history of the Scylding kings.

The use of Frothi as a typical usurper in the English Waldef story is also a very strong indication that the story in which he has his proper setting was current in England; otherwise, by what channel did he get into the Waldef story?[132]

Our next question is, What stories of the "exile-return" type were current in the portions of England in which the Hroar-Helgi story would naturally circulate? We think, of course, immediately of *Havelok the Dane*. Deutschbein has shown that *Havelok* is founded on historical events that occurred in the first half of the tenth century.[133] The gist of the story is that an heir to the Danish throne is deprived of his heritage, suffers deep humiliation, but finally regains his heritage and, through marriage, the crown of Norfolk in England in addition. The story was of a nature to make a strong appeal to the Scandinavians, especially the Danes, in England. It achieved, in fiction, the ambition which the Danes realized under Swen and Canute, when these sovereigns governed both Denmark and England. It was a Danish story; it was developed after 950, which was about the time the third stage in the development of the Hroar-Helgi story had been reached; and it was a creation of the Scandinavians in England, among whom the story circulated.

Closely connected with the Havelok story is the Meriadoc story, the first part of which, as Deutschbein has shown,[134] and in regard to which J.D. Bruce agrees with him,[135] is based on the Havelok story. These stories Deutschbein calls "cymrisch-skandinavische Sage" and says, "Wir sehen, dass den Cymren und den Skandinaviern in England der wesentliche Anteil an der Entwicklung unserer Sage zukommt."[136]

It is evident that in the Havelok and Meriadoc stories we have every condition present for contact between them and the Hroar-Helgi story, namely: time (after 950); place (England); people among whom all the stories would circulate (Scandinavians, coming in contact with the Welsh); and, in the case of the Havelok and Hroar-Helgi stories, a popular theme dealing with Danish princes who regain a lost kingdom. The theme would be all the more popular as the time when the Havelok story was developed was a period of struggle on the part of the Scandinavians in the British Isles to gain and maintain supremacy.[137] Again, the nature of the Hroar-Helgi story was such that its development depended wholly on invention or on contact with other stories.

The first part of the Meriadoc story, with which a comparison will be made, is summarized by J.D. Bruce as follows:—

"In the time of Uther Pendragon, Caradoc ruled over Wales. He had a son and a daughter by his wife, a princess of Ireland, which country he had conquered. As old age approaches, he turns over the government of his kingdom to his brother Griffith and devotes himself to hunting and amusement. Wicked men persuade Griffith to slay his brother and seize the throne. Despite the warning of a dream, Caradoc goes hunting and is slain by hired assassins in the forest.

"The queen dies of grief, and, to turn suspicion from himself, Griffith has the assassins put to death. Before their execution, however, they revealed Griffith's guilt. Caradoc's friends among the nobles wish to get out of Griffith's power their late master's children, who had been committed to the charge of Ivor and Morwen, the royal huntsman and

his wife. Griffith determines to kill the children, but, touched in a measure by their appeal, does not have them executed on the spot. He has them taken to the forest of Arglud, where they are to be hanged. The executioners, however, feel compassion and tie them by a slender rope, easily broken, so that they may fall to the ground unharmed. Hearing of the children's disappearance, Ivor sets out for the forest, accompanied by his wife and his dog, Dolfin. To frighten the executioners away, he kindles fires in the four quarters of the forest and throws flesh into these fires to attract the wolves. He then hides himself in a tree. The wolves gather and the men, afraid, conceal themselves in the hollow of the tree to which the children had been hanged. Ivor drives away the wolves and then begins to smoke out the men. They promise to give up the children, if he will let them come forth. He consents, but kills them one by one, as they are crawling out.
"He delivers the children, who have been suspended for half a day, and flies with them and his wife and dog to the Fleventanean forest. Here he takes refuge in a caverned rock, called Eagle Rock, because there were built on it the nests of four eagles who constantly faced the four points of the compass. How Ivor and his wife struck fire from flint, and the peculiar way in which they cooked their food is described. One day Urien, King of Scotland, passing through the forest, carries off the girl from her companion, Morwen. Similarly Kay, Arthur's seneschal, carries off the boy from Ivor. Morwen goes to Scotland to seek Orwen, the girl; Ivor to Arthur's court to seek Meriadoc, the boy.
"The day Morwen reached Scotland, Urien and Orwen are to be married. The latter recognizes Morwen in the throng by the wayside and has her brought to the palace. Ivor comes with a dead stag to Arthur's court and offers it to Kay. Meriadoc recognizes his foster-father and springs clear over the table to greet him. Kay receives Ivor among his attendants. Kay visits Urien and takes Ivor and Meriadoc with him. Mutual recognitions and rejoicings.
"Arthur and Urien determine to take vengeance on Griffith, who fortifies himself at Mount Snowdon. After a long siege he succumbs to famine, surrenders and is executed. Meriadoc succeeds him, but resolves to leave Urien in charge of the kingdom and go forth in search of adventure."[138]

According to Saxo's version of the Hroar-Helgi story, the usurper procures the assassination of his brother and, to avoid suspicion, has the assassins put out of the way. In this the Meriadoc story agrees. In *Meriadoc*, the queen dies of sorrow. No mention is made of the queen in Saxo's version. In the Hamlet story, the brother slays the king with his own hand, but secretly, to avoid suspicion. He marries the king's widow. In the *Hrlfssaga*, the brother attacks the king with an army and slays him. In *Havelok*, Arthur, likewise, attacks the king with an army and slays him.[139] The widow is rescued. In the *Hrlfssaga*, as appears at the end of the story, the widow is not only rescued, but, as in the Hamlet story, marries the usurper.

In *Meriadoc*, the murdered king's adherents try to rescue the young prince and princess. This feature is common to both the *Hrlfssaga* and Saxo's version of the Hroar-Helgi story. In *Meriadoc*, the usurper gets the children into his power, but, being appealed to, saves them for the time being. This feature is found in Saxo's version, where the usurper agrees to spare the children during good behavior. It is lacking in the *Hrlfssaga*. In *Meriadoc*, the usurper plans to have the children hanged in a forest. In Saxo's version, the children having violated the condition on which they are to be spared, the usurper gathers an army to attack them. In the *Hrlfssaga*, there is a continuous effort on the part of the usurper to make away with the children.

In *Havelok*, Grim, a fisherman, rescues the prince, who lives as a fisherman's son, under the name of Cuaran. In *Meriadoc*, the royal huntsman, Ivor, rescues the children and they live in a cave in the woods as a huntsman's children; Ivor is accompanied by his wife and his dog, Dolfin. In the *Hrlfssaga*, the children live in a cave in the woods as a shepherd's (Vifil's) children, responding, when necessary, to the names of dogs. In Saxo's version of the Hroar-Helgi story, the children are concealed in a hollow tree, food being brought to them under the pretence that they are dogs, and dogs' names are applied to them. In the Hamlet story, the rescue is supplied by the insanity motive, but friends at court are not wanting.

There is no insanity in *Meriadoc* or *Havelok*; but it is present in the *Hrlfssaga* and Saxo's version of the story about the two boys. In the *Hrlfssaga*, the boys, especially Helgi, cut crazy capers while on the way with Svil when he goes to Frothi's hall in response to an invitation. Helgi rides horseback with his face to the horse's tail, just as Hamlet does; and the horse is an untamed colt, the idea coming from the fact that, when Hamlet is thus riding, a wolf appears and one of the men, to test his sanity, calls the wolf a colt. It would, indeed, be an untamed colt. In Saxo's version, better use is made of the insanity motive. Pretended insanity is the only resort left the boys to save themselves. In the *Hrlfssaga*, it serves no other purpose than to attract attention to the boys and reveal their identity to Signy and Svil.

In *Havelok*, the prince returns home, and, with the aid of a faithful friend, Sigar, who has remained at court, the usurper is overthrown and the crown regained. In *Meriadoc*, Arthur and Urien besiege the usurper, starve him out, and execute him. Meriadoc becomes king. In the Hamlet story, the prince returns from England, whither the usurper has sent him in order to get rid of him, sets fire to the hall in which the usurper's men lie drunk after a feast, and goes to the usurper's chamber and slays him. Nothing is said about the queen, though the presumption is that she perishes also. In the *Hrlfssaga*, the boys, aided by their foster-father and brother-in-law, trusty friends, set fire to the hall in which the usurper's men lie drunk after a feast; and the usurper's egress through an underground passage having been blocked, he perishes in the flames. The queen, the boys' mother, refusing to leave the hall, perishes also. In Saxo's version, the boys attack the usurper in his hall and set fire to the building; he hides himself in a secret underground passage and perishes of smoke and gas.

It is told of Ivor that when he rescues the children he is accompanied by his dog. Not only that, but the dog's name is given. This looks as if some use is to be made of the dog; otherwise there is no point in the statement that a dog is present, whose name is Dolfin. Bruce says, "It is to be remembered that even this Welsh version, no doubt, passed through the hands of a French romancer before reaching the author of our Latin text";[140] and there is reason to suspect that this is one of the places where the story has suffered. Both Saxo's version of the Hroar-Helgi story, and the *Hrlfssaga*, show to what use a dog's name could be put; and this specific reference to the dog in *Meriadac*, and the use that might have been made of him in an earlier version of the story, arouse a strong suspicion that here is the source of the suggestion of using dogs' names in the Hroar-Helgi story to aid in saving the boys. Even if no such use was ever made of the dog in the Meriadoc story, such specific reference to him is in itself very suggestive. That the Hroar-Helgi story employs two dogs' name's is, of course, due to the fact that there are two boys to which they are to be applied, although, so far as the plot is concerned, the matter could have been managed with the use of one dog's name; and the fact that the dogs' names, in the *Hrlfssaga*, are Hopp and Ho, and that the boys' later assumed names are Hrani and Hamur, is due to a desire to preserve the initial letter, "H," of their names, which is in accordance with Scylding nomenclature.[141]

Furthermore, in the *Hrlfssaga* it is said that Vifil concealed the boys in a cave in the woods. Likewise, in *Meriadoc*, Ivor concealed the boy and the girl in a cave in the forest. But in Saxo's version of the Hroar-Helgi story, the boys are concealed in a hollow tree. This also must be an adaptation from *Meriadoc*. The men who were to execute the prince and princess hanged them on the branch of a large oak-tree (quercus) and concealed themselves inside the tree, which was hollow. Ivor, in an attempt to rescue the children,

"Quatuor igitur ingentes focos e quatuor partibus ipsius saltus accendit, accensisque plurimas quas secum attulerat carnes passim iniecit ilicemque uicinam cum coniuge et cane ascendens delituit. Fumo autem ignium per nemoris latitudinem diffuso, ubi lupi in confinio degentes—quorum inibi ingens habebatur copia—odorem perceperunt carnium, illo contendere et confluere ilico coeperunt."[142]

Here we have the idea of a hollow oak with people in it, wolves in the vicinity, and children at hand who have been hanged, and therefore presumably dead. Had the cord broken by which they were hanged, they would certainly have been torn to pieces by the wolves. But especially striking is the statement that Ivor's dog is concealed in a tree; and this tree is called "ilex" (holly-oak), the very word used by

Saxo to designate the kind of hollow tree that Hroar and Helgi (he calls them Harald and Halfdan, as has been stated) are concealed in, under the pretence that they are dogs. Also, pieces of meat are thrown into the fires; and Ivor, as soon as the men in the hollow tree beg for mercy, shoots four wolves and "ceteri omnes lupi in eos qui uulnera pertulerant irruerunt eosque membratim dilacerantes discerpserunt."[143] Here is again the idea of meat for wolves and the bodies of animals torn asunder. The idea of dismembered bodies of children is indeed absent; but the whole passage in *Meriadoc* is so suggestive of what we find in Saxo, even to the hiding of a dog, whose name is given, in an "ilex," that it would be remarkable if there was no connection between Saxo's story and *Meriadoc*.

Again, as has already been stated, Saxo says that Frothi perished in an underground passage, of smoke and gas. The men who, in *Meriadoc*, were to execute the prince and princess concealed themselves in a hollow tree, which had an entrance that was so formed that "depressis humeris, illam necesse erat subire,"[144] which is suggestive of the stooping that would probably be necessary in entering an underground passage. But what is noteworthy in this connection is that, at the entrance to the tree, Ivor starts a fire "cuius calore fumique uapore inclusos pene extinxit."[145] Saxo says that Frothi "Vbi dum clausus delitescit, uapore et fumo strangulatus interiit."[146] Here is the idea of concealment again, but particularly noteworthy is the suffocation by "uapore et fumo," the same words that are used in *Meriadoc*. In the *Hrlfssaga*, the account of the events immediately preceding Frothi's death resembles more the account of the corresponding events in the Hamlet story than does Saxo's account; but in the *Hrlfssaga* also, Frothi attempts to escape by an underground passage.

The use of wolves' claws and the dismembered bodies of children to mislead those who might seek to get possession of the boys is the employment, as Deutschbein has observed, of a form of deceit similar to that practiced by Joseph's brethren.[147]

In regard to the manner in which the children are saved, it is difficult to correlate the Hroar-Helgi story with the Meriadoc story as definitely and simply as one would wish, but the explanation probably lies in the following idea expressed by Bruce, "In conclusion, as to this division there seems to be a certain confusion of *motifs* in the first part of the *Historia Meriadoci* with regard to the manner in which the children are saved from execution."[148] The statement, for instance, that the children were suspended for half a day is out of all harmony with the statement that they were to be suspended by slender ropes, easily broken, that would permit them to fall to the ground unharmed. But Bruce's statement quoted above, "This Welsh version, no doubt, passed through the hands of a French romancer before reaching the author of our Latin text," would account for the "confusion of *motifs*"; and the fact that we have not now that form of the story with which the Hroar-Helgi story came in contact would obscure some of the points of relationship between the two. But the hiding of a dog, whose name is given, in an oak tree of a particular species (ilex) is so definite and unique a point of identification that there is no mistaking it.

But even if we had the Meriadoc story in its original form, we should not expect to find it exactly reproduced in the Hroar-Helgi story. Various causes would operate to introduce changes. Such features as mountain-rocks with their eagle-nests would be modified to bring the topography more into harmony with that of Denmark, so that the caverned rock would naturally become an earth-cave. Characteristics of Scandinavian life and history would supplant what was peculiarly Welsh. Thus the shrewd old shepherd, Vifil, naturally takes the place of the royal huntsman, Ivor; and Saxo, quite naturally, gives the story a marked Danish geographical and historical setting, which he does by introducing such names as Fyen and Seeland, and by connecting the Danish royal family in the beginning of the story with those of Sweden and Gautland.

Allowance must also be made for two lines of oral transmission, one going to Iceland, and the other to Norway and thence to Denmark. This would result in the modification of details in the two versions, such as details connected with the insanity motive and the concealment of the boys, and the omission, in one version, of the dogs' names supposed to be applied to the boys and the insertion of the names in the other.

But this would not explain why Hroar, Helgi, and their father are given other names in Saxo's version, and why such a radical change has been made in the family relationship of Siward and Signy. This, however, as will be explained later,[149] is due to arbitrary action on the part of Saxo, in order to conceal the fact that he twice includes the same group of men in his line of Danish kings.

If the foregoing is substantially correct, much in the Hroar-Helgi story is accounted for, besides some striking differences between the two versions. But it is possible to account for more. We have seen how the Siward story exerted marked influence on the story about Bothvar Bjarki; hence, we might expect it to have exerted some influence on the Hroar-Helgi story, which is also a part of the *Hrlfssaga*. And this it has done. Siward was historically closely associated with the events of the Macbeth story; but the Macbeth story is of a type that, in one noteworthy particular at least, resembles the Hroar-Helgi story more than do any of the stories thus far considered, and that is in the fact that Duncan has two sons, who flee when their father is murdered. In the Macbeth story, as in the Hamlet story, it may be said that we have not, under a strict interpretation of the term, an instance of the "exile-return" type of story; but Hamlet goes to England and immediately upon his return avenges his father's murder, and, still nearer the type, Malcolm and Donaldbane flee and Malcolm returns and avenges his father's murder. But the matter of type is, in this connection, unessential. There is no doubt that the Hamlet story exerted an influence on the Hroar-Helgi story, nor can there be any doubt that the Macbeth story did the same.

First, attention is called to the fact that in the *Hrlfssaga* Siward himself is retained in the story under the name of Svil.[150] In Saxo's version of the story about Hroar and Helgi, he is called Siward, but there his proper relationship to the other characters is obscured. Siward was related to Duncan by marriage, some versions, Holinshed's for instance, having it that Duncan was married to Siward's daughter;[151] similarly, Svil was married to Halfdan's daughter. Siward aided Duncan's sons (Donaldbane, however, not being present to take part in the expedition against Macbeth); similarly, Svil aided Halfdan's sons, not by an armed expedition against Frothi, the usurper, but proceeding against him in such manner as the plot of the story permits. It is said of Donaldbane, that he fled to Ireland "where he was tenderlie cherished by the king of that land";[152] similarly, Hroar went to Northumberland, where he received a hearty welcome and later married King Northri's daughter, gn.[153] Siward was first an earl in Denmark; similarly, Svil was an earl in Denmark. Svil did not, however, become Earl of Northumberland, as Siward did; but Hroar took his place, so to speak, in this respect, and, as Siward had done, married the earl's (king's) daughter[154] and became King of Northumberland.

In the Hroar-Helgi story, the usurper is represented as consulting a witch in regard to the whereabouts of the young princes. This feature must also be due to the influence of the Macbeth story; for, though the purpose for which Frothi and Macbeth consult the witch, or witches, is not exactly the same, it is the possible future disposition of the throne that in both instances causes anxiety; and while at first, in both instances, a prediction, or information, is given that is favorable, a prediction in both instances is given in conclusion that is unfavorable. The witches are so conspicuous a feature of the Macbeth story that they would, of course, attract the attention of the saga-man; and we naturally expect this feature of the story to leave its impress on the Hroar-Helgi story. It is a special feature, not found in any of the other stories considered in this connection, and there can be no doubt as to whence the Hroar-Helgi story acquired it. The witch in the saga is called a "seikona." Concerning the kind of witchcraft practised by a "seikona," P.A. Munch has the following: "Som den virksomste, men og som den skjendigste, af al Troldom ansaa vore Forfdre den saakaldte *Seid*. Hvorledes den udvedes, er ikke ret klart fremstillet ...; den var forbunden med sang ... Men dette slags Troldom ansaaes ogsaa en Mand uvrdigt, og udvedes derfor sdvanligviis af Kvinder, ligesom dette ogsaa stedse synes at have gaaet ud paa noget ondt."[155] Thus the "seikona" is exactly the same kind of creature as the witches in the Macbeth story. Consider, for instance, the disgusting practice in which Shakespeare represents them as engaging, as they go round the cauldron, chanting the refrain, "Double, double toil and trouble," *etc*. W.J. Rolfe refers to the witches in *Macbeth* as follows: "Macbeth and his fellow captain Banquo have performed prodigies of valour in the battle, and are on their way home from the field when they are met by the three witches, as Shakespeare calls them, and as they are called in the old chronicle from which he took the main incidents of his plot. They appear simply to be the witches of superstition—hags who have gained a measure of superhuman knowledge and power by a league with Satan, to whom they have sold their souls and pledged their service."[156] The statements at an earlier stage of the story in the *Hrlfssaga*, while the boys are still on the island, that soothsayers and wise men are called in from all over the land to tell where the boys are, and that wizards, who are also summoned, warn Frothi to beware of the old man Vifil on the island, remind us of the statement by Holinshed that Macbeth "had learned of certeine wizzards, in whose words he put great confidence ... how that he ought to take heed of Macduffe."[157]

Still another feature may have been acquired from the Macbeth story. It is said that Hroar and Helgi were transferred to a neighboring island. Holinshed says that Donaldbane fled to Ireland. The Macbeth story has been treated by a number of chroniclers, who, though they agree in the main, occasionally disagree in regard to details. Thus Johannes Fordun says, "Hi a Machabeo rege expulsi, Donaldus insulas, Malcolmus Cumbriam adibant."[168] This is evidently one version and would supply the hint for transferring the young princes to a neighboring island, which would be a convenient disposition to make of them till the time of their return to regain their heritage. It would also harmonize topographically with the coast of Denmark, where there were many islands covered with trees, the idea of woods as a hiding-place for the boys having been abundantly supplied by the Meriadoc story.

It may be said that this introduces a conflict with the statement that Donaldbane fled to Ireland. It is not possible to know, in a case like this, which variant has influenced the saga, or whether, indeed, both have not been utilized. But there was ample warrant for transferring Hroar to Northumberland without such a suggestion as lay in Donaldbane's flight to Ireland. In any event, imitation of Donaldbane's flight has not been a necessary consideration in making Hroar King of Northumberland. A suggestion of the same nature lay in Hamlet's going to England, where he married the king's daughter; but chiefly, the Scandinavians were numerous in the north of England and regarded themselves as the rightful possessors of that part of the country. The mastery of Northumberland was long an object of contest between Anglo-Saxons and Scandinavians, and this was the chief point at issue in the famous battle at Brunanburh, 937. Since Helgi, whom the *Hrlfssaga* represents as the more forward of the two boys, was made King of Denmark, no more honorable disposition could be made of Hroar than to place him on the throne of Northumberland, and events show that he himself was perfectly satisfied. He thus also became ruler of the land once governed by Siward, who must have made a powerful impression on his countrymen in England; and with one of the two princes reigning in Denmark and the other in England, the glory of the Danes when Canute was king of both countries would be revived in story, as it was in *Havelok the Dane*, where Havelok, likewise, reigned both in England and Denmark.

No attempt has been made to point out all the respects in which the Hroar-Helgi story resembles the Macbeth story. The Macbeth story has most of the characteristics of the "exile-return" type, and striking resemblances that fall in with features of the stories already mentioned might have been added, but will suggest themselves to the reader. Only such things as point to special influence exerted by the Macbeth story on the Hroar-Helgi story have been mentioned.

It may be urged that some of the material, such as the "seikona," said in the foregoing to be derived from foreign sources, is recognized saga-material. The point, however, is that it is not the material itself, but the suggestion for the use of it, that in such an instance is said to be derived from a foreign source.

The Hroar-Helgi Story in the SKJ[O.]LDUNGASAGA_ and the *BJARKARMUR.*

Thus far nothing has been said about the "short and chronicle-like form in the Icelandic *Skj[o.]ldungasaga*, where the fratricide is called Ingjald, not Frothi."[159] The story is, in substance, as follows.

Fridleif, King of Denmark, abducted Hilda, daughter of Ali, King of the Uplands in Norway, and by her had a son who was named Ali; by another woman he had a son who was named Frothi.

Frothi inherited his father's kingdom; but Ali, his half-brother, who was a great warrior, conquered Sweden. Frothi's men feared Ali and persuaded Frothi to try to have him put to death. Frothi yielded to their entreaties, and Starkad, the famous warrior, was dispatched to perform the deed. When an opportunity presented itself, he stabbed Ali to death. "My brother has caused this," said Ali, and died laughing.

Later, Frothi defeated Jorund, King of Sweden, and made him a tributary prince. He also defeated Swelling, a Swedish duke, and treated him in the same manner. Frothi abducted Jorund's daughter, by whom he had a son who was called Halfdan. But taking another woman to wife, a legitimate heir was born to him, and this son was called Ingjald.

Starkad, however, was so filled with remorse for having killed Ali that he did not wish to remain with Frothi. He went, therefore, soon after to Russia and later to Sweden, but, disgusted with the idolatry of the Swedes, returned to Frothi. Ingjald, son of Frothi, had in the meantime married the daughter of Swerting, thus, as it seemed to all, effecting a reconciliation with him.

Jorund and Swerting, however, formed a conspiracy against Frothi, and he was slain one night while sacrificing to the gods. In the meantime, Starkad was absent in Sweden, where, under the guise of friendship, he was detained by gifts, in order that the plot against Frothi might be the more easily executed.

Swerting placated Ingjald, Frothi's son and Swerting's son-in-law; but Halfdan, Ingjald's half-brother, conquered Skne and avenged his father's murder by putting to death Swerting's twelve sons, who had slain Frothi. At the instigation of Starkad, Ingjald put his wife, Swerting's daughter, aside. He also granted Halfdan a third of the kingdom. Swerting's daughter later bore Ingjald a son (Agnar); and by his wife, Sigrith, Halfdan had a daughter, Signy, and two sons, Hroar and Helgi.

Ingjald, however, desiring to rule over the whole kingdom, fell upon Halfdan unexpectedly with an army and slew him. He married Halfdan's widow, and by her had two sons, Hrrik and Frothi. Signy grew up under her mother's care, and later Ingjald gave her in marriage to Svil, an earl in Seeland. But Hroar and Helgi hid from the king on an island near Skne, and when they had arrived at the proper age they slew Ingjald and thus avenged their father's death.

Hroar and Helgi now became Kings of Denmark. Later Hroar married the daughter of the King of England. Hrolf, nicknamed Kraki, who was eight years old when his father, Helgi, died, succeeded him on the throne. Hroar was soon after slain by his half-brothers, Hrrik and Frothi. Hrolf then became sole King of Denmark.[160]

The story in the *Bjarkarmur* is substantially the same as the story in the *Skj[o.]ldungasaga*. Both are plainly based on the same account, and, within certain limits, are identical with the corresponding story in the *Hrlfssaga*. Skne, mentioned in the *Skj[o.]ldungasaga* in the phrase "in insula quadam Scani," is not mentioned in the *Hrlfssaga*. Its insertion in the *Skj[o.]ldungasaga* is due to the fact that Halfdan, the father of Hroar and Helgi, is said to have conquered Skne, and, as a result, would be regarded as having ruled there. But its presence in one account and omission in the other involve no contradiction. In all that belongs peculiarly to the story about Hroar and Helgi, the account in the *Skj[o.]ldungasaga* is identical with the account in the *Hrlfssaga*. According to both sources, the name of the boys' mother was Sigrith; their father's name was Halfdan; he was slain by his brother, who fell upon him unexpectedly with an army; the fratricide married the murdered man's widow; Signy was the sister of Hroar and Helgi; she married Svil, an earl in Denmark; Hroar and Helgi had to conceal themselves on an island to save their lives (according to the *Bjarkarmur*, they were brought up by the old man Vifil, a circumstance omitted in the *Skj[o.]ldungasaga*, but contained in the *Hrlfssaga*); when they had arrived at the proper age, they slew (according to the *Hrlfssaga* and the *rmur*, "burnt-in") their father's murderer and thus avenged their father's death; Hroar and Helgi then became Kings of Denmark; Hroar married the daughter of the King of England; Helgi's son was Hrolf, who later became sole King of Denmark.

The essential difference between the story as it is in the *Skj[o.]ldungasaga* and as it is in the *Hrlfssaga* is that, in the *Skj[o.]ldungasaga*, Ingjald is said to be the brother of Halfdan; while in the *Hrlfssaga*, Frothi is Halfdan's brother. The *Hrlfssaga* has, however, preserved the earlier account. The *Skj[o.]ldungasaga* dates from about the year 1200.[161] About the year 950, Frothi is said to be the slayer of Halfdan;[162] and in *Historia Regis Waldei*, Frothi is made the typical villain in a Hroar-Helgi type of story[163] (the "exile-return" type), so that, in the version of the story that was current in England, Frothi must have been the slayer of his brother. The conflicting statement that it was Ingjald who slew Halfdan requires, therefore, an explanation.

In Saxo's *Gesta Danorum*, the story about Hroar and Helgi is told twice. It is first told in the second book, where we find the version with which is connected the story about Hrolf Kraki, Yrsa, Athils, and Ingjald and his son Agnar, whom Bjarki slew; it is told a second time in the seventh book, where Hroar and Helgi are called Harald and Halfdan, and where the story about them is another version of the same story that we have in the *Hrlfssaga*. Not only do Hroar and Helgi appear (disguised under different names), but Frothi and Ingjald again appear.

A comparison of the line of Danish kings as Saxo has it, with the line of the same kings in the *Skj[o.]ldungasaga*,[164] shows that the *Skj[o.]ldungasaga* has the story about Hroar and Helgi just where Saxo's second story about them (i.e., in his seventh book) puts in its appearance. These lines of kings are as follows:—

SAXO: SKJ[O.]LDUNGASAGA:

Humblus I
Dan I
Humblus II
Lotherus
Scioldus Scioldus
Gram
Swibdagerus
Guthormus
Hadingus
Frotho I
Haldanus, Roe, Scatus
Roe, Helgo
Roluo Krage
Hiartwarus
Hotherus
Balderus
Roricus
Vigletus
Wermundus
Uffo
Dan II
Hugletus
Frotho II
Dan III
Fridleus I Fridleifus I[165]
Frotho III[166] Frotho I[166]
Herleifus
Havardus
Leifus
Herleifus[167]
Hunleifus[167]
Aleifus[167]
Oddleifus[167]
Geirleifus[167]
Gunnleifus[167]
Frotho II
Vermundus
Dan I
Dan II[168]
Hiarnus[169] Frotho III
Fridleus II[170] Fridleifus II
Frotho IV Frotho IV
Ingellus Ingjaldus, Halfdanus

Olauus[171]
Frotho V, Haraldus[172] Agnerus, Roericus, Roas or Roe, Helgo
Haraldus,[173] Haldanus,[174] Frotho (V)[175] Rolpho Krag

A comparison of the two lines of kings shows that, beginning with the first Fridleus in Saxo's account and the first Fridleifus in the *Skj[o.]ldungasaga's* account, there are important correspondences. Fridleus I (Saxo) = Fridleifus I (*Skjs.*). Frotho III, son of Fridleus I (Saxo) = Frotho I, son of Fridleifus I (*Skjs.*). Fridleus II, son of Frotho III (Saxo) = Fridleifus II, son of Frotho III (*Skjs.*). Frotho IV (Saxo) = Frotho IV (*Skjs.*); and in both sources Frotho IV is the Danish king in whose career Swerting plays such a prominent part. By omitting all of Saxo's kings between Scioldus and Fridleifus I, among whom are also the Hroar-Helgi group, the *Skj[o.]ldungasaga* has avoided the difficulty of having to deal with Hroar, Helgi, and Hrolf Kraki where they first occur in Saxo's history.

The paralleling of the two lines of kings also furnishes the key to the explanation of how the different names and a different setting for the Hroar-Helgi story, from those found in other versions, got into Saxo's version. Since the Hroar-Helgi story appears in the same place in his line of kings as in that of the *Skj[o.]ldungasaga*, he must also have known the names that really belonged to the story. But he had told the story about Halfdan, Hroar, Helgi, and Hrolf Kraki (in its second stage of development, see p. 66) once before, and therefore could not consistently tell a different story about the same men. The story was, however, in existence and was too good to be discarded, so he retained it, but disguised it by making arbitrary changes. This explains the loss, which otherwise would be very strange, of such well known names as Hroar, Helgi, and Hrolf Kraki. The only incentive any one could have to change the names would be just that which Saxo had, namely that he had used them before in another connection. He retained the name Frothi, which appears so often in the Danish line of kings that its reappearance would cause no difficulty; and his retention of Frothi as the slayer of his brother is additional evidence that to him, not to Ingjald, was this unenviable rle first assigned. Ingjald, whom he has in his story about Hrolf Kraki, he also retained, but in a different relationship from that in his second book. It will be observed that Saxo merely shifted the name Halfdan from father to son, and that Harald, almost a conventional name, he employed twice. Finally, he introduced a strange person, Olaf, about whom, he says, nothing, practically, was known.

But since Saxo has the Hroar-Helgi story substantially as it is in the *Hrlfssaga*, except for the changed names, the author of the *Skj[o.]ldungasaga*, or its source, whose version of the story occurs in the same place in the line of Danish kings as Saxo's, must also have known the story in the same version. This we shall find was actually the case, and that the story as it appears in the *Skj[o.]ldungasaga* is an attempt at reconciling conflicting elements in ancient tradition.

As already stated, according to the *Grottas[o.]ngr* (from about 950), Frothi is the brother of Halfdan and slays him. But according to an equally old tradition, the story on which the Ingjald lay in Saxo's sixth book is based, Frothi is Ingjald's father and is himself slain. The events that gave rise to this lay are also narrated in Saxo's sixth book and are as follows.

In Saxony were two kings, both of whom paid tribute to Frothi. They planned to throw off the foreign yoke. Hanef made the attempt first, but Frothi defeated and slew him. Swerting made the attempt later and slew Frothi, but met his own death at the same time. Swerting's sons, fearing that Ingjald would avenge his father's death, gave him their sister in marriage. Thus a reconciliation was effected, and Ingjald thenceforth devoted himself to pleasure. Starkad, the famous warrior, who was in Sweden, had been one of Frothi's men and had later been Ingjald's foster-father. When Starkad learned that Ingjald, instead of seeking revenge, had made friends with his enemies and had taken Swerting's daughter to wife and with her was leading a life of luxury, the old warrior hastened back to Denmark. When Starkad returned, Ingjald's wife, not knowing him on account of his shabby appearance, insulted him. Ingjald was away on a hunt at the time; but when he returned, he recognized Starkad and told his wife who the old man was. In the evening Ingjald sat down to a luxurious meal with Swerting's sons; and his wife did all she could to appease Starkad, who was also present. But Starkad could not forget the insult he had suffered, and became more and more angry with the effeminate way of living that Ingjald and his wife had introduced from Germany. In burning words, which are reproduced in the Ingjald lay, he condemned Ingjald's neglect of duty, his luxurious mode of life, and his living in friendship with those on whom he should have avenged his father's death. Ingjald was finally aroused, and he drew his sword and killed all of Swerting's sons. In regard to his future relation to his wife Saxo says nothing; but as Starkad advised him to drive the impudent woman (as he called her) from the land, the presumption is that Ingjald did so.

The Ingjald lay has its roots in *Beowulf.* Its relationship to the corresponding episode in the Anglo-Saxon poem is explained in the following by Olrik:—

"Kun et eneste af Starkad-digtningens mange optrin kan flges til ldre kilde end de nordiske. Det er den scene, hvor den gamle kriger opgger Ingjald til hvn og dermed afbryder forsoningen imellem de to fjendtlige slgter. I *Bowulf* findes dette optrin for frste gang, ganske afvigende i den politiske stilling, men med kendeligt slgtskab i det digterske indhold.

"Digtet fortller on det forsg der blev gjort p at stille den lange fejde, der var frt mellem Danernes folk og Hadbardernes, af Halvdan og Hrodgar imod Frode og Ingeld. Forsoningen skulde frembringes ved bryllup mellem Ingeld og Hrodgars datter Freyvar (Fraware). 'Hun blev lovet, ung og guldsmykt, til Frodes hulde sn; det bar tyktes Skjoldungers ven s, rigets vogter (i.e., Hrodgar) har fundet det rdeligt, at ved den viv skulde tvisten og ddsfejden stilles. Ofte, ej sjlden, hviler dog ddsspyddet kun fje tid efter mandefald, hvor gv s bruden er. Da m det mistykke Hadbardernes drot og hver thegn af det folk, nr ban gr med jomfruen i hallen, at en hirdsvend af Danerne sknked for skaren; ti p ham strler fdrenes eje, hrdt og ringlagt, Hadbardernes klenodier, slnge de ejede de vben (indtil de misted i skjoldelegen de kre fller og deres eget liv). Da mler ved llet en gammel spydkmpe, der ser skatten, og mindes al mndenes undergang; grum er hans hu. Fuld af harm begynder ban at friste en ung kmpes hu med hvad der bor i hans bryst: "Kender du, min ven, denne klinge, som din fader bar til svrdstvnet sidste gang—dette kostelige jrn—dengang Danerne slog ham; de beholdt valpladsen, de raske Skjoldunger; siden kom der aldrig oprejsning efter kmpernes fald. Nu gr her afkom af de banemnd her i hallen, pralende af skattene, bryster sig af drabet, brer det klenodie som du med ret skulde eje!"—Sledes maner og minder han atter og atter med srende ord, indtil den stund kommer, at jomfruens svend segner blodig ned for klingens bid, skilt ved livet for sin faders dd; men den anden (i.e., drabsmanden) undflyr levende, han kender vel landet. Da brydes fra begge sider dlingernes edspagt; i Ingeld koger ddshadet, men krligheden til hans viv klnes efter den harm. Derfor kalder jeg ikke Hadbardernes trofasthed, deres del i folkefreden, svigels mod Danerne, deres venskab ikke fast.'[176]

"Trods den antydende stil i digtets fremstilling, sledes som den lgges helten Beovulf i munden, er handlingens sammenhng nogenlunde tydelig. Der bar vret gammel fejde mellem Daner og Hadbarder; hvis man kan tro betydningen af et ikke helt sikkert ord, er ogs Hadbardernes konge (Frode) falden i striden. Ingeld, Frodes sn, slutter fred med Danernes konge Hrodgar og holder bryllup med hans datter. Under selve bryllupet blusser kampen op, idet en af brudesvendene bliver drbt af en af Hadbarderne, som en gammel kmpe bar gget op til at hvne sin faders dd. Bryllupet (og drabet) foregr—efter digtets fremstilling—snarest i Hadbardernes kongehal; ti det hedder, at drabsmanden undslap fordi ban kendte landet. Ingelds rolle er indskrasnket til at hans krlighed til kongedatteren 'klnes'; at hun er bleven forskudt eller selv er vendt hjem, fremgr deraf, at hun i digtet gr i den danske kongehal som ugift og sknker for kmperne.

"Kampen nvnes en gang til, i *Bowulfs* begyndelse, dr hvor det hedder on den danske kongehal Hjort: 'den opleved fjendske ildblger, hrjende lue; det var ikke lnge efter at kamphadet vgned efter [gammelt] ddsfjendskab mellem svigersn og svigerfader.'[177] Disse ord—der nppe stammer fra den egenlige Bowulfdigter—indeholder en afvigende fremstilling: bryllupskampen str i den danske kongehal, og synes at vre opfattet som strre og voldsommere end en enkelt mands mord og hans banemands undslipning. At sagnet vakler med hensyn til stedet, er ikke s underligt. Historiske forhold viser, at bryllup snart er holdt i svigersnnens, snart i svigerfaderens hjem.

"Ogs Wds-kvadet taler on en kamp 'i Hjort' (t Heorote), hvor Ingeld og hans Hadbarder skal have lidt et nederlag mod Hrodgar og hans brodersn Hrodulf. Det er rimeligst, at ogs dette er hentydning til det blodige bryllup, opfattet p lignende mde og henlagt til samme skueplads som i den nysnvnte antydning.

* * * * *

"Handlingen foregr i Ingelds kongehal, og indholdet er at en gammel kmpe bevger en ung til i selve hallen at drbe snnen af sin faders banemand, herved blusser det gamle fjendskab mellem folkene op, og Ingeld forskyder sin udenlandske hustru.

"Forskellen er den, at i *Bowulf* er faderhvneren en fra Ingeld forskellig person. Dette er sikkert det ldre, og Ingjaldskvadets det yngre. Det glder som en lov for episk udvikling, at man arbejder sig hen imod det enklere; hvis to personer udfrer beslgtede handlinger, vil den ene af dem forsvinde; og i kraft af digtningens midtpunktsgen, vil bifiguren g ud af spillet, hans rolle vil enten blive til intet eller overtages af hovedpersonen. Digtningen har gjort et stort skridt frem i episk ttning, da Ingeld blev bde faderhvner og den der forskd sin hustru; det hele drama udspilles nu imellem den unge konge og den gamle stridsmand.

* * * * *

"Episk er omdannelsen naturlig nok; nationalt er den meget mrkeligere. Det er ikke s underligt, at den ldre form handler om Daner og Hadbarder, den yngre om Daner og Sakser. Men det overraskende er, at Hadbardernes parti gres til 'Daner' og de tidligere Daner til 'Saksere'; den danske heltetradition er her ganske vildfarende i, hvem der er folkets egne forfdre, og hvem der er dets bitreste fjender. Dog ogs dette bliver episk forklarligt. Bevidstheden om Hadbarderne, der engang havde fyldt Danerne med rdsel, svandt efterhnden bort, fordi stersegnenes hele tniske stilling forandredes. Ikke en eneste gang er deres navn overleveret i samtlige den nordiske literatur! Men hvor synskres og navne glemmes, drages personer og optrin nrmere til. Efter Vendernes indvandring til sterskysten bliver alle dens gamle

sagnhelte opfattede som Danske: Anglernes Offa, Hadbardernes Ingeld, Holmrygernes Hagena. Senere i tiden flytter ogs andre af den gotiske verdens store sagnskikkelser nordp: minder om Hunnerslaget overfres p Danmarks sydgrnse (Dan, Fredfrode); Volsunger, Nibelunger, Didrikskmper—alle blev til en eller anden tid gjorte til vore landsmnd, efter ganske samme nrhedslov, hvormed Nordmndene gjorde danske kmper som Starkad og Bjarke til norske helte. I og for sig er der intet mrkeligere i, at Ingeld og den opggende gamle spydkmpe gres til Daner. Som *Bjarkeml* blev udgangspunkt for ganske uhistoriske forestillinger on Skjoldungttcn, sker det ogs her—i endnu strre mlestok. Ingjaldsk vadet bar bortkastet alt det historiske stof, undtagen den gamle kmpes harmtale, og det skaber en ny episk sammenhng, som det gennemfrer paa glimrende mde.
"Nu forstaar vi Ingelds nationalitetsskifte. Det mrkelige er blot, at de oprindelige Daner blev gjorte til Saksere. Men ogs, dette flger af den episke udvikling. Nr den gamle kmpe er det punkt der tiltrkkes (fordi han er det poetiske tyngdepunkt), m hans modparti frastdes og gres til Danefolkets fjender. Nogen selvstndig betydning ejer denne part jo ikke.

> "Udtalt i jvnere ord vil dette sige, at man i vikingetiden tog et gammelt sagnstof og deri fandt udtryk for sin tids store oplevelse, sammenstdet mellem Danmark og et mgtigt 'saksisk' rige.[178]

"Det eneste nye navn, vi mder, er betegnelsen 'Svertings snner.' I ldre digtning (*Bowulf*) er 'Svertings tling' Geaternes konge; men da bevidstheden on 'Geaterne' blegnede, er navnet vel sprunget over og er knyttet til en kendt folkestamme, Sakserne. Grunden dertil er muligvis kun, at det danner bogstavrim med Sakser, og at det sproglig har en biklang af sort, *i.e.*, ond og listig, der gjorde det egnet til at bruges om Danernes fjender."[179]

The significance of this is, first, that in the Ingjald lay we are dealing with old material; secondly, that the account of the relationship in the *Skj[o.]ldungasaga* between Frothi and Swerting and their families is based on the Ingjald lay; thirdly, that when the nationality of Swerting and those associated with him is changed from Saxon to Swedish, it is merely another stage in the development of the story, quite in line with earlier changes made to keep the story in harmony with changing conditions.

Thus we have two stories, based on the same events (events first related in *Beowulf* and *Widsith*), that come down to posterity by two independent lines of transmission and suffer changes in the course of time that bring them into absolute conflict with each other. According to both stories, Frothi has become a Danish king. But in the story connected with the Ingjald lay, Frothi is slain, and is avenged by his son, Ingjald; while in the *Hrlfssaga*, Frothi is his brother's slayer, on whom vengeance is taken by the sons (Hroar and Helgi) of his victim (Halfdan). In the *Skj[o.]ldungasaga*, the conflict is obviated. It is done very deftly and with only such disturbances of the genealogical relations involved as seemed necessary to secure the desired result. As a consequence, the changes that have been made, for which, in most instances, the reasons are quite apparent, can be traced step by step. The story as we have it in the *Skj[o.]ldungasaga* is, therefore, plainly an artificial amalgamation designed principally to harmonize conflicting stories about Frothi.

The genealogy in the *Skj[o.]ldungasaga* is as follows:—

```
Swerting   Frothi
Jorund
|       |  |                                         |
|       |  |
daughter
|       |  |_________________________________________|
|       |                                          |
daughter   Ingjald          Sigrith
Halfdan
|        |  |             |  |                       |
|________|  |_____________|  |_______________________|
|          |   |                  |         |      |
|          |   |                  | [180]   |      |
Agnar   Hrrik  Frothi  Eng.  Lady Hroar    Helgi   Signy
Svil
|        |         |      |    |
|________|         |      |____|
|
Hrolf Kraki
```

Below is the same genealogy with the portions enclosed that, on the one hand, are taken from the Ingjald lay (Frothi, Swerting, *etc.*) and, on the other, from the *Hrlfssaga* (Halfdan, Sigrith, *etc.*). The names in italics are found in the *Hrlfssaga*, but, with the exception of gn, whose name is omitted altogether, are employed in another connection in the *Skj[o.]ldungasaga* (see the foregoing table):—

```
.------------------.
Swerting   Frothi
Jorund
|       |  |                                       |
|       |  |
daughter
|       |  |_______________________________________|
|       |                                        |
```

```
|       |                 .------------------------------
------.
|       |                                               |
daughter   Ingjald        Sigrith   Frothi[181]
Halfdan
|         |  |           |  | |____|                 |
|________|  |___________|  |__________________________|
|         |    |              |         |        |
`-----------------'        |                    |        |
|
|         |     |              |         |        |
Agnar   Hrrik  Frothi Eng.  Lady Hroar   Helgi   Signy
Svil
(gn)    |        |        |     |
|________|        |       |_____|
|            |             |
|            |             |
Agnar   Hrolf Kraki     Hrok
`-----------------------------------'
```

It will be observed that the following changes have been made to produce the family relationship as we find it in the *Skj[o.]ldungasaga*. Frothi is removed as Halfdan's brother and becomes his father, a change suggested, probably, by the tradition related in Saxo's second book that Frothi was Halfdan's father, and facilitated by the fact that, in the *Hrlfssaga*, the father of Halfdan and Frothi is not mentioned, and, as a result, presents no impediment to the change. But to explain how Halfdan has become Frothi's son, a new relationship has to be invented, so Frothi is said to have the son Halfdan by the daughter of Jorund. According to the *Hrlfssaga*, Halfdan is slain by his brother. This idea, in the abstract, is retained. But, according to the new arrangement, Ingjald, Frothi's son, has become Halfdan's brother, *i.e.*, half-brother; hence, Ingjald slays Halfdan. According to the *Hrlfssaga*, Halfdan's brother and slayer marries his widow, Sigrith.[182] This idea is also retained. In the *Hrlfssaga*, it is Frothi who slays his brother, Halfdan, and marries his widow, Sigrith. But, according to the new arrangement, Ingjald is Halfdan's brother and slayer; hence, it is now he who marries Sigrith. According to the *Hrlfssaga*, Agnar is Hroar's son; but this, apparently, is not according to current tradition. According to Saxo's second book, he is Ingjald's son and is slain by Bjarki. This conception of him occurs in the *Hrlfssaga* also, but towards the close, where Bjarki, in recounting his own achievements, mentions his having slain Agnar. This Agnar is not Hroar's son, but the Agnar of the *Skj[o.]ldungasaga* and of Saxo's second book. The *Skj[o.]ldungasaga*, therefore, properly retains him as Ingjald's son and omits him as Hroar's son. Hrok and Hrrik are the same person. According to the *Hrlfssaga*, he is the son of Svil and Signy. Olrik has about a page of comment on him,[183] in which he shows that he (Hrethric, Hrothgar's son, in *Beowulf*) was originally regarded as Hroar's son, but, for reasons that need not here be rehearsed, became a fluctuating character. The *Skj[o.]ldungasaga* has made him the son of Ingjald. In the *Hrlfssaga*, Hroar is said to have married an English lady named gn. The *Skj[o.]ldungasaga* also says that Hroar married an English lady, but omits her name.

Finally, Ingjald is given another son, Frothi. He corresponds to Frothi V in Saxo. In Saxo, however, Frothi is the slayer of his brother and corresponds to the Frothi who appears in the *Hrlfssaga* as the slayer of Halfdan. As the Frothi who appears in the *Hrlfssaga* becomes, in the *Skj[o.]ldungasaga*, the father of Halfdan, and Ingjald becomes Halfdan's slayer, Frothi, Ingjald's son, is, as a consequence, assigned the rle of joining his brother Hrrik in slaying his half-brother Hroar. Thus the idea of Frothi (corresponding to Frothi V in Saxo) as a fratricide is retained. But as Ingjald is succeeded on the throne by Halfdan's sons, Hroar and Helgi, there is no opportunity for Ingjald's son Frothi to become king. It will also be remembered that Frothi IV in the *Skj[o.]ldungasaga*, who, like Frothi IV in Saxo, was slain by Swerting (or his sons), was himself a fratricide, having caused the death of his brother Ali. Frothi IV in the *Skj[o.]ldungasaga* corresponds to the Frothi mentioned in the *Hrlfssaga*. Thus, as a fratricide, Frothi IV in the *Skj[o.]ldungasaga* corresponds to the Frothi in the *Hrlfssaga*, and as the victim of Swerting, he corresponds to Frothi IV in Saxo; while the account of Frothi, Ingjald's son, as the slayer of his half-brother Hroar, preserves the idea that Frothi V (in Saxo) is his brother's slayer. The *Skj[o.]ldungasaga* has, therefore, amply retained the idea of Frothi as a fratricide, and contains an account that, in a way, embraces the essential features of the treatment of the same period in the *Hrlfssaga*, on the one hand, and in Saxo, on the other. The relationship in the *Skj[o.]ldungasaga* of Frothi (Ingjald's father), Swerting, Ingjald, and Swerting's daughter is identical with that in the Ingjald lay.

Thus we see how, at the most conspicuous and interesting juncture of the Danish royal line, the *Skj[o.]ldungasaga* harmonizes conflicting traditions.[184] This involves a train of consequences, among which are the following:—

1. "The short and chronicle-like form [i.e., of the Hroar-Helgi story] in the *Skj[o.]ldungasaga*, where the murderer is called Ingjald, not Frothi," is taken from the account that appears in the *Hrlfssaga*; this account must therefore be earlier than the corresponding account in the *Skj[o.]ldungasaga*.

2. As the story about Frothi, Halfdan, *etc*., in the *Bjarkarmur* is substantially the same as in the *Skj[o.]ldungasaga*, it must be derived from the same source as the story in the *Skj[o.]ldungasaga*. The *Bjarkarmur* are, therefore, at this point a later composition than the corresponding portion of the *Hrlfssaga*; and this fact affords further corroboration of the idea that the stories in the *rmur* of Bjarki's slaying the wolf and Hjalti's slaying the bear are later than the *Hrlfssaga's* account of Bjarki's slaying the winged monster.

3. When the *Skj[o.]ldungasaga* says that Hrolf Kraki met Hrani-Odin on the expedition to Sweden, though nothing is said about such a meeting in *Snorri's Edda*, the idea is probably taken from a version of the story essentially as we have it in the *Hrlfssaga*.[185]

4. Though the *Hrlfssaga* is made up of elements of varying degrees of antiquity and merit, it contains features worthy of more consideration than has generally been accorded them.

5. In discussing the genealogy of the Danish kings in *Beowulf* and comparing it with that of other documents,[186] it is to be remembered that the *Skj[o.]ldungasaga* has no independent value as an authority in this connection; its value lies in its recognition of a conflict between the Ingjald lay and the story in the *Hrlfssaga*, and its attempt to harmonize the two.

6. On the whole, as Olrik says, "Hvor vrdifuld den islandske *Skj[o.]ldungasaga* end er, den er selvflgelig ikke p alle punkter at foretrkke for enhver anden kilde."[187] When it disagrees with other documents, its statements should be scanned with care.

A little ought to be said about Saxo's treatment of the problem, the solution of which in the *Skj[o.]ldungasaga* has just been considered. The solution in the saga is based on the recognition of the fact that Frothi as a king who was slain (i.e., by Swerting) and later avenged by his son is irreconcilable with the idea that he slew his brother, whose sons later put Frothi to death and thus avenged their father's murder. Saxo solved the problem by employing two Frothi's,—namely Frothi IV, Ingjald's father, who was slain by Swerting and was avenged by his son, and Frothi V, Ingjald's successor, who slew his brother, Harald (i.e., Halfdan in the *Hrlfssaga*), and later was put to death by Harald's sons.

On the whole, Saxo's story presents something of an attempt to harmonize Danish and Old Norse tradition. The Danish tradition about the Hroar-Helgi group of kings Saxo preserves in his second book. The Old Norse tradition about them he utilizes in his seventh book, at a point where, in the line of Danish kings, it occurs according to the Old Norse conception of the matter.[188] In the latter connection he repeats certain features of the story as it appears in his second book. Ingjald who appears in the sixth book is really the same Ingjald (second book) whose son Agnar is slain by Bjarki; and Helgi (here called Halfdan) takes to sea, just as he does in the second book. All that concerns Hrolf Kraki, Yrsa, Bjarki, *etc.*, Saxo omits from the seventh book; but he gives Halfdan (Helgi) a career in Sweden, something like Helgi's (second book). Halfdan dies, however, without leaving an heir to the Danish throne; and this solves another problem, for thus the necessity of introducing Hrolf Kraki, Helgi's son, again, or some substitute for him, is obviated, and the story of this royal family is brought to an end.

Conclusion.

We have, therefore, only two versions of the Hroar-Helgi story (Saxo's version and the one in the *Hrlfssaga*), and these have been subjected to a variety of influences and manipulations. The two versions do not, however, always employ the same features in just the same way, as is exemplified in the treatment of the insanity motive; nor have they always retained the same features present in the source of influence, as where the place of concealment of the boys in one instance is a cave and in the other a hollow tree. But the possession of the two versions is valuable in this respect, that they afford a double confirmation of the source of influence, as in the instances just cited and in Frothi's consulting the witch.

It is a great transformation that has taken place in the fortunes of Hrothgar (Hroar) from the time we become acquainted with him as the famous King of the Danes in *Beowulf* till we finally see him in the *Hrlfssaga* sitting on the throne of Northumberland in England. But the conception of him that excludes him from the list of ancient kings of Denmark seems to have been shared by Snorri Sturlason; for in Snorri's *Ynglingasaga*, where Frothi, Halfdan, Helgi, Hrolf Kraki, and other early Danish kings are mentioned, and where one would expect something to be said about Hroar also, his name does not occur and there is no reference to him whatever.

The foregoing explanation of how Hroar came to be regarded as King of Northumberland has a bearing on *Beowulf*-criticism. The name of Hroar's wife is given as gn. In *Beowulf*, Hrothgar's wife, Wealhtheow, is called a Helming and is supposed to be an English lady. In support of this idea, Sarrazin[189] and, following him, Thomas Arnold[190] have stated that perhaps we have a reminiscence of her nationality in that of gn. But, as we have seen, there is no connection between the two women.

Finally, let it be stated that not all has been said about the Hroar-Helgi story that one would like to say. One would like to be able to trace still more in detail the development of the story and account for all the variations between the two versions. Such knowledge is, however, vouchsafed in very few instances. But if what has been said is substantially correct, a little has been added to what was known before about this interesting story.

III

GENERAL SUMMARY.

From what has been said, it will be seen that the origin of the dragon in the *B[o.]varsttr* of the *Hrlfssaga* has hitherto been unperceived and the story of Bjarki's fight with the dragon has not been understood. Neither of the two has any connection with *Beowulf.* The *Bjarkarmur* throw no light on the *Beowulf* problem, for the story of Bjarki's slaying the wolf and that of Hjalti's slaying the bear are later than the story of Bjarki's slaying the dragon and were written by one who had the story of Bjarki's fight with the dragon in mind. Moreover, the story told in the *rmur* in connection with Hjalti's slaying the bear is merely an adaptation of the story told in the *Hrlfssaga* about Bjarki's father.

The *Frattr* of the *Hrlfssaga* embodies an earlier form of the Hroar-Helgi story than is found in the *Skj[o.]ldungasaga* and the *Bjarkarmur*; and this confirms the idea that the story in the *Hrlfssaga* of Bjarki's fight with the winged monster is earlier than the corresponding stories in the *Bjarkarmur.* Aside from the influence exerted by the Hamlet story, the *Frattr* version and Saxo's version of the Hroar-Helgi story are the result of influences emanating from the "exile-return" type of story in England, and, nore particularly, the Meriadoc story and the Macbeth story, which were well known to Scandinavians in Great Britain.

The version of the Hroar-Helgi story which we find in the *Skj[o.]ldungasaga* and the *Bjarkarmur* is the result of an attempt to harmonize conflicting traditions emanating from events about which we now find the first account in *Beowulf* and *Widsith*, as is also Saxo's treatment of the same matter in his sixth and seventh books.

The change of names in Saxo's version of the Hroar-Helgi story is the result of arbitrary action on his part in order to conceal the fact that he introduces into his history the Hroar-Helgi group of kings a second time, namely in his seventh book, and gives an account of them that conflicts with the account already given of them in his second book.

INDEX

FOOTNOTES:

[Footnote 1: For these portions of the *Bjarkarmur*, see pp. 47-48.]

[Footnote 2: For the story of Bjarki's fight with the winged monster, see pp. 20-22.]

[Footnote 3: See p. 51.]

[Footnote 4: *Ant. Tid.*, 1852-54, p. 130.]

[Footnote 5: *Ang.*, 1886, IX, pp. 198-201.]

[Footnote 6: *P.B.B.*, 1887, XII, pp. 55-57.]

[Footnote 7: *Beow. Stud.*, 1888, pp. 62-63.]

[Footnote 8: *Beow. Unt. Ang.*, 1889, p. 55.]

[Footnote 9: *Beow. Unt.*, 1888, pp. 185-88.]

[Footnote 10: *Eng. Stud.*, 1892, XVI, p. 80.]

[Footnote 11: The list is "Osbern Thruwin Aeskitil Riculf Aeskyl Rikui Boduwar Berki Esel Petre Osbern."]

[Footnote 12: *P.B.B.*, 1895, XX, pp. 157-58.]

[Footnote 13: *Eng. Stud.*, 1897, XXIII, pp. 243-46.]

[Footnote 14: *Notes, Beow.*, 1898, p. 96.]

[Footnote 15: *Grundr.*, 1898, III, p. 649.]

[Footnote 16: *Ark.*, 1903 (the article is dated 1901), XIX, pp. 19 ff.]

[Footnote 17: *Oldn. Lit. Hist.*, II, 1901, p. 832.]

[Footnote 18: *Helt.*, I, 1903, pp. 135-36.]

[Footnote 19: *Helt.*, I, p. 135.]

[Footnote 20: *Helt.*, I, pp. 139-41.]

[Footnote 21: *Helt.*, pp. 215-17.]

[Footnote 22: *Helt.*, I, p. 248.]

[Footnote 23: *Hrs. Bjark.*, 1904, Introd., p. 22.]

[Footnote 24: *Eng. Stud.*, 1905, XXXV, pp. 19 ff. The similarity between "Gullinhjalti," in the *Hrlfssaga*, and "gylden hilt," in *Beowulf*, was first pointed out by Friedrich Kluge in *Englische Studien*, 1896, XXII, p. 145. Sarrazin would write "gylden hilt," the form in which the words appear in *Beowulf*, in one word and capitalize it (i.e., Gyldenhilt). This manner of writing the words brings them nearer in form to "Gullinhjalti," as this word is written in the *Hrlfssaga*. Holthausen in his latest edition (1909) of *Beowulf* also uses the form "Gyldenhilt." Lawrence, likewise, identifies "gylden hilt" with Gullinhjalti (see p. 12), as does also Panzer (see p. 12).]

[Footnote 25: *St. Sag. Eng.*, 1906, pp. 249 ff.]

[Footnote 26: *Camb. Hist. Lit.*, I, 1907, pp. 29-30.]

[Footnote 27: *Gesch. Alteng. Lit.*, 1908, p. 993.]

[Footnote 28: *P. M. L. A.*, 1909, XXIV, p. 237.]

[Footnote 29: *P. M. L. A.*, XXIV, p. 239.]

[Footnote 30: *P. M. L. A.*, XXIV, p. 231.]

[Footnote 31: *P. M. L. A.*, XXIV, p. 231.]

[Footnote 32: *P. M. L. A.*, XXIV, p. 224.]

[Footnote 33: *P. M. L. A.*, XXIV, p. 223.]

[Footnote 34: *P. M. L. A.*, XXIV, p. 224.]

[Footnote 35: *St. germ. Sag.*, 1910, pp. 366 ff.]

[Footnote 36: *St. germ. Sag.*, pp. 372-73.]

[Footnote 37: *St. germ. Sag.*, p. 383.]

[Footnote 38: XVIII, pp. 318-19.]

[Footnote 39: See the legendary life of Siward in the following.]

[Footnote 40: *Ark.*, XIX, p. 199.]

[Footnote 41: Olrik, *Ark.*, XIX, p. 205.]

[Footnote 42: *Ark.*, XIX, pp. 212-13.]

[Footnote 43: *Ark.*, XIX, pp. 205-07. See also *Helt.*, I, pp. 215-17. In his *St. germ. Sag.*, p. 378, n., Panzer calls in question the connection that Olrik makes between Bjarki's bear-ancestry and that of Siward. But Olrik's theory furnishes the only satisfactory explanation of all the phenomena involved, and is so extremely probable that it must be regarded as correct.]

[Footnote 44: *Hrs. Bjark.*, pp. 59-60.]

[Footnote 45: *Sn. Ed.*, pp. 107-10.]

[Footnote 46: See p. 95, 3 and note.]

[Footnote 47: *Ark.*, XIX, p. 211]

[Footnote 48: *Helt.*, I, p. 136.]

[Footnote 49: *St. germ. Sag.*, p. 367.]

[Footnote 50: *P. M. L. A.*, XXIV, p. 239.]

[Footnote 51: *Hrs. Bjark.*, pp. 68-71. Lawrence's translation of the above is as follows:—

"And as the Yule-feast approached, the men grew depressed. Bothvar asked Hott the reason; he told him that a beast had already come two successive winters, a great and terrible one,—'and it has wings on its back and flies about continually; two autumns it has already sought us here, and it does great damage; no weapon wounds it, but the king's champions, the best warriors of all, don't come home at this time.' Bothvar said, 'The hall isn't so well defended as I thought, if a beast can destroy the domain and property of the king.' Hott answered, 'That is no beast, it is rather the greatest of monsters.' (at er ekki dr, heldr er at hit mesta tr[o.]ll). Now came the Yule-even; and the king said, 'Now I desire that the men be still and quiet in the night, and I forbid them all to run any risk on account of the beast; let the cattle fare as fate wills (sem aunar); my men I do not wish to lose.' All promised to act as the king commanded. But Bothvar crept secretly out in the night; he made Hott go with him, but Hott only went because he was forced to, crying out that it would surely be the death of him. Bothvar told him it would turn out better. They went out of the hall, and Bothvar had to carry him, so full of fear was he. Now they saw the beast, and Hott shrieked as loud as he could, and cried that the beast was going to swallow him. Bothvar commanded the dog (bikkjuna hans, *i.e.* Hott) to keep still, and threw him down in the moss, and there he lay in unspeakable terror, and didn't even dare to run home. Then Bothvar attacked the beast, but it chanced that the sword stuck in the sheath when he wanted to draw it; then he pulled so hard at the sword that it flew out of the sheath, and he plunged (leggr) it immediately with such force under the shoulder of the beast that it penetrated the heart, and hard and heavily fell the beast down on the ground dead. Then Bothvar went over to where Hott was lying. He took him up and carried him over to the place where the beast lay dead. Hott trembled frightfully. Bothvar said, 'Now you must drink the blood of the beast.' For a long time he was loth to do this, but he finally didn't dare to do otherwise. Bothvar made him drink two big gulps, and eat some of the beast's heart; then Bothvar grappled with him, and they struggled long with each other. Bothvar said, 'Now you have become very strong, and I don't believe that you will be afraid of the troop of King Hrolf any longer.' Hott answered, 'I shall not fear them any more, nor shall I be afraid of you henceforth.' 'That is well, comrade Hott,' [said Bothvar] 'and now will we set up the beast, and arrange it so that the others will think it alive.' They did so. Then they went in and were quiet; no one knew what they had done.

"The king asked in the morning whether they knew anything of the beast; whether it had showed itself anywhere in the night; they told him the cattle were all safe and sound in the folds. The king bade his men see if they couldn't find any indication that it had come thither. The warders obeyed, came quickly back again and told the king that the beast was advancing rapidly to attack the town (borginn). The king bade his men be courageous, [and said] each one should help, according as he had courage for it, and proceed against this monster. It was done as the king commanded; they made themselves ready for it. The king looked at the beast and said, 'I don't see that the beast moves; but who will undertake the task and attack it?' Bothvar answered, 'A brave man might be able to satisfy his curiosity about this! (at vri nsta hrausts manns forvitnisbt.) Comrade Hott, destroy this evil talk about you,—men say that there is neither strength nor courage in you; go up and kill the beast!—you see nobody else wants to.' 'Yes,' said Hott,'I will undertake it.' The king said. 'I don't know whence this courage has come to you, Hott, you have changed marvellously in a short time.' Hott said, 'Give me your sword Gullinhjalti, which you are bearing, and I will kill the beast or die in the attempt.' King Hrolf said, 'This sword can only be borne by a man who is both brave and daring.' Hott answered, 'You shall be convinced that I am such a man.' The king said, 'Who knows whether your character hasn't changed more than appearances show? Take the sword and may you have good fortune!' Then Hott attacked the beast and struck at it as soon as he was near enough so that he could hit it, and the beast fell down dead. Bothvar said, 'Look, lord, what he has done!' The king replied, 'Truly he has changed much, but Hott alone didn't kill the beast, you were the man who did it.' Bothvar said, 'It may be so.' The king said, 'I knew as soon as you came here that only few men could compare with you, but this seems to me your most illustrious deed, that you have made a warrior out of Hott, who appeared little born to great good fortune. And now I wish him called Hott no longer, he shall from this day be named Hjalti,—thou shalt be called after the sword Gullinhjalti.'"—P.M.L.A., XXIV, pp. 226-27.]

[Footnote 52: *Ark.*, XIX, pp. 207-08.]

[Footnote 53: See p. 7.]

[Footnote 54: *Gratis.*, p. 92.]

[Footnote 55: *Sc. Folkl..*, p. 65.]

[Footnote 56: *Sc. Folkl..*, p. 66.]

[Footnote 57: *Sc. Folkl..*, p. 108.]

[Footnote 58: *Sagn.*, p. 34.]

[Footnote 59: *Event. Sagn..*, p. 10.]

[Footnote 60: *Event. Sagn..*, pp. 52-53.]

[Footnote 61: "Ebbe svarede, at trolde kmpede ved nar."—*Helt..*, I, p. 126. The sunlight is represented as being invariably fatal to trolls.]

[Footnote 62: George Webbe Dasent says (*Pop. Tales*, Introd., pp. 57-58): "The trolls, or, the other hand [i.e., in comparison with the Giants], with whom mankind had more to do, were supposed to be less easy tempered, and more systematically malignant, than the Giants, and with the term were bound up notions of sorcery and unholy power.... But when Christianity came in, and heathendom fell; when the godlike race of sir became evil demons instead of good genial powers, then all the objects of the old popular belief, whether sir, Giants, or Trolls, were mingled together in one superstition, as 'no canny.' They were all trolls; all malignant; and thus it is that, in these tales, the traditions about Odin and his underlings, about the Frost Giants, and about sorcerers and wizards, are confused and garbled; and all supernatural agency that plots man's ill is the work of Trolls, whether the agent be the arch enemy himself, or giant, or witch, or wizard."

It is quite impossible to characterize trolls in detail with unqualified words or phrases. They are usually malignant, though there are instances of their doing men a good turn. They are always very powerful, and are usually very large. It is told of one troll that, had she not made a misstep, she would have succeeded in wading from Norway to Iceland; and of another, that the thumb of his glove held four bushels, good measure. In some instances, however, it is possible for many trolls to enter one room of an ordinary dwelling house. There are trolls with three heads, with six heads, with nine heads, and with twelve heads. Sometimes they are one-eyed, and sometimes they have other characteristics that differentiate them from human beings. In fact, anything with supernatural qualities is apt to be called a troll. As a rule, it is impossible for human beings to cope with trolls except by outwitting them, which often is done. They are inimical to Christianity; and, though their depredations may occur on any day of the year, between sunset and sunrise, adventures with trolls, as stated above, are frequently represented as occurring Christmas Eve; and that is the time when particular precaution must be taken to avoid them. Usually it is taken for granted that trolls will not attack the inmates of a house, and people feel perfectly safe so long as they do not venture out. In another type of troll story, however, people expect trolls to invade the house Christmas Eve and attack them; and to avoid injury, the inmates vacate the house for the night, before sunset. Illustrations of these statements are found in such well known collections of fairy tales as *Sc. Folkl.*, *Nor. Tales*, *Folk. Huld. Even.*, *Event. Sagn.*]

[Footnote 63: This story is in print and was related to the present writer by one who had read it; and, though diligent search has failed to locate it again, the writer ventures to reproduce it, for he is certain that it is in existence.]

[Footnote 64: *Folk. Huld. Even.*, Pt. I, pp. 66ff.]

[Footnote 65: *St. germ. Sag.*, pp. 367-68.]

[Footnote 66: "Dette hallen hjemsgende uhyre."—*Hrs. Bjark.*, Introd., p. 22.]

[Footnote 67: *Icel. Leg.*, pp. 140 ff.]

[Footnote 68: That it was the cattle of King Hrolf that the dragon attacked has been recognized by others, Mllenhoff (*Beow. Unt. Ang.*, p. 55) and Chadwick (*Camb. Hist. Lit.*, I, p. 29), for instance; but they make no more of the matter than to state it correctly.]

[Footnote 69: *Grettis.*, pp 92 ff.]

[Footnote 70: *Folk. Huld. Even.*, Pt. II, pp. 53 ff.]

[Footnote 71: *Helt.*, I, pp. 117-18.]

[Footnote 72: *P. M. L. A.*, XXIV, p. 239.]

[Footnote 73: *St. germ. Sag.*, p. 366.]

[Footnote 74: *St. germ. Sag.*, p. 368.]

[Footnote 75: *St. germ. Sag.*, p. 372.]

[Footnote 76: See pp. 11-12.]

[Footnote 77: *Beow. Unt. Ang.*, p. 55.]

[Footnote 78: *Beow. Unt.*, p. 187.]

[Footnote 79: *Helt.*, I, p. 135.]

[Footnote 80: *Nor. Tales*, p. 366. The sword here in question is just like the sword in Grendel's cave in *Beowulf*, except that it is not said to have a golden hilt.]

[Footnote 81: Other tales which contain the motive that a strength-giving drink enables one to wield a sword that has supernatural qualities are: *The Big Bird Dan* and *The Seven Foals* (*Nor. Tales*, pp. 266 and 449); *The Three Brothers* (Polish, *Yel. Fair. Bk.*, p. 144); and *Lonkenlus* (*Event. Sagn*, p. 268). It may be urged that in all these instances the drinking imparts strength, not bravery. But the two qualities are closely related; and the saga-man makes it plain that, by means of the drink, Hott has acquired both. Bothvar says, "Now you have become very strong, and I don't believe that you will be afraid of the troop of King Hrolf any longer." Hott answers, "I shall not fear them any more." Later Bothvar says, referring to the proposed attack on the propped-up dragon, "A brave man might be able to satisfy his curiosity about this! Comrade Hott, destroy this evil talk about you,—men say that there is neither strength nor courage in you; go up and kill the beast!" "Yes," says Hott, "I will undertake it." The king says, "I don't know whence this courage has come to you, Hott, you have changed marvellously in a short time." From the foregoing and what is said about Hott's wrestling with Bothvar, it is plain that the author has taken particular pains to emphasize the fact that, by partaking of the heart and blood of the dragon, Hott has acquired great strength, the lack of which seems to have been the cause of his cowardice. It seems equally plain that when Hott knocks over the dead propped-up dragon by means of the sword Gullinhjalti, which the king explicitly says "can only be borne by a man who is both brave and daring," the purpose is to call particular attention to the fact that it is by wielding the sword that Hott gives proof of the change that has come over him. Regardless of the deceit that has been practiced in connection with the dead dragon, the king is compelled, if he believes what he has said about Gullinhjalti, to recognize that Hott has demonstrated by his ability to wield the sword that he is now "a man who is both brave and daring." And the king does recognize it, for he says to Bothvar, "You have made a warrior out of Hott."]

[Footnote 82: *Hrs. Bjark.*, p. 100.]

[Footnote 83: Ll. 1557, 1567, 1607, 1666.]

[Footnote 84: Ll. 1558, 1569, 1605, 1615, 1663, 1696.]

[Footnote 85: Ll. 1559, 1573.]

[Footnote 86: Ll. 1564, 1616, 1667.]

[Footnote 87: L. 1697.]

[Footnote 88: *Eng. Stud.*, XXXV, p. 22.]

[Footnote 89: L. 1697.]

[Footnote 90: Ll. 1573-74.]

[Footnote 91: "The chief of the Weder-Geats took no more of the treasure-holdings in the dwelling, though he saw many there, but only the head, and with it, the sword's hilt, brave with gold; the sword had already melted" (ll. 1612-15).—*Beow.*, Child.]

[Footnote 92: "I bore the hilt thence away from my enemies" (ll. 1668-69).]

[Footnote 93: "Then the golden hilt, the work of giants long ago, was given into the hand of the old prince, the white-haired battle-leader" (ll. 1677-79).—*Beow.*, Child.]

[Footnote 94: "Hrothgar spake, looked on the hilt, the old heirloom, on which was written the beginning of that far-off strife, when the flood, the streaming ocean slew the giant kind—they had borne themselves lawlessly. The people were estranged from the Eternal Lord; the Wielder, therefore, gave them their requital through the whelming of the waters. So was it duly lined in rimed staves on the guard of gleaming gold, set down and told for them for whom that sword was wrought, choicest of blades, with twisted hilt and decked with dragon-shapes." (LI. 1687-93).—*Beow.*, Child.]

[Footnote 95: L. 1687.]

[Footnote 96: L. 1698.]

[Footnote 97: "He gave the guardian of the boat a sword ornamented with gold" (ll. 1900-1901).]

[Footnote 98: "Then the shield of earls, the king stout in battle, bade fetch Hrethel's sword, mounted in gold; there was not then among the Geats a better treasure in the like of a sword. He laid it on Beowulf's lap." (ll. 2190-94).—*Beow.*, Child.]

[Footnote 99: *Mort. d'Arth.*, p. 480.]

[Footnote 100: "En l'orie pont assez i at reliques."—*Ext. Ch. Rol.*, p. 103.]

[Footnote 101: "Preditum auro capulum."—*Gest. Ḋan.*, p. 118.]

[Footnote 102: See pp. 31 ff.]

[Footnote 103: *St. germ. Sag.*, p. 370.]

[Footnote 104: *St. germ. Sag.*, p. 372.]

[Footnote 105: *Eng. Nov.*, p. 2.]

[Footnote 106: *Hrs. Bjark.*, pp. 139-40 and 141-42. Lawrence's translation of the above selections from the *rmur* is as follows:—

"Most of the men insulted Hjalti; he was not clever in speech. One day they (Bjarki and Hjalti) went out of the hall, so that the king's men did not know of it. Hjalti was afraid, and cried, 'Let us not go near this wood; there is a she-wolf here, which eats men; she will soon kill us both.' The she-wolf burst out of a thicket, frightful, with gaping jaws. Hjalti thought this terrible; his legs and all his limbs trembled. Undaunted Bjarki advanced upon her, struck deep with his axe; fearful blood streamed from the she-wolf. 'Between two things,' said

Bothvar, 'shall you choose, Hjalti,—drink this blood, or I will kill you, no courage seems to be in you.' Angrily answered Hjalti, 'I don t dare to drink blood; (but) it is best to do it if I must; now I have no better choice.' He lay down to drink the blood; then he drank three swallows,—enough for fighting with one man! His courage increased, his strength waxed, he became very strong, mighty as a troll, all his clothes burst open. So he became courageous at heart, he feared not the flight of steel, the name of coward he feared no more, he was equal to Bothvar in courage." (IV, 58-66.)

"He (Hjalti) has gained a brave heart and a courageous disposition; he has got strength and valor from the blood of the she-wolf. The folds at Hleidargard were attacked by a gray bear; many such beasts were there far and wide thereabout. Bjarki was told that it had killed the herdmen's dogs; it was not much used to contending with men. Hrolf and all his men prepared to hunt the bear—'he shall be greatest in my hall, who faces the beast!' Roaring the bear ran from its lair and shook its baleful paws, so that the men fled. Hjalti looked on when the combat began; he had nothing in his hands. Hrolf tossed to Hjalti his sword; the warrior stretched forth his hand and grasped it. Then he plunged it into the bear's right shoulder, and the bear fell down dead. That was his first heroic deed, many others followed; his heart was ever brave in the battle. From this exploit he got the name of Hjalti the brave, and was the equal of Bjarki." (V, 4-13.)—*P. M. L. A.*, XXIV, pp. 229-30.]

[Footnote 107: *Helt.*, I, p. 118.]

[Footnote 108: When, here and elsewhere in this discussion, the *Hrlfssaga* is referred to as an earlier composition than the *Bjarkarmur*, the implication is not intended that the version of the saga which we now have was earlier committed to writing.]

[Footnote 109: See p. 51.]

[Footnote 110: *St. germ. Sag.*, p. 367.]

[Footnote 111: *Beow. Unt. Ang.*, p. 55.]

[Footnote 112: *Beow. Unt.*, p. 186.]

[Footnote 113: *Helt.*, I, p. 116.]

[Footnote 114: *St. Sag. Eng.*, p. 250.]

[Footnote 115: *Gest. Dan.*, p. 56. Elton's translation of the passage is as follows: "When he was triumphing in these deeds of prowess, a beast of the forest furnished him fresh laurels. For he met a huge bear in a thicket, and slew it with a javelin; and then bade his companion Hjalti put his lips to the beast and drink the blood that came out, that he might be the stronger afterwards. For it was believed that a draught of this sort caused an increase of bodily strength."—*Elton's Saxo*, p. 69.]

[Footnote 116: See pp. 36 ff.]

[Footnote 117: See, for instance, *Sc. Folkl.*, p. 253, where dragons are said to have been pierced "under their shoulders to the heart."]

[Footnote 118: Finnur Jnsson has also been struck by the similarity between the story connected with Bjarki's birth and the second story in the *rmur*, in which Hjalti slays a bear. He says, "I rimerne (V, 5-14) er der endnu tale om en 'grbjrn.'"—*Hrs. Bjark.*, Introd., p. 22.]

[Footnote 119: *Hrs. Bjark.*, Introd., p. 18.]

[Footnote 120: See p. 16.]

[Footnote 121: The dogs are here said to be the herdsmen's dogs, in conformity with the spirit of the story in its new setting and to differentiate the story from what it is in the place whence the author of the *rmur* took it.]

[Footnote 122: *Hrs. Bjark.*, Introd., p. 22.]

[Footnote 123: See pp. 50 ff.]

[Footnote 124: For further proof of this, see pp. 81 ff.]

[Footnote 125: See p. 11.]

[Footnote 126: In the foregoing no implication is intended as to the identity of the story of Beowulf's fight with Grendel and Saxo's story of Bjarki's slaying the bear. The result, however, of the discussion is to establish the priority of Saxo's story to that in the *Hrlfssaga*; hence, an attempt to identify Bjarki's exploit with Beowulf's exploit must consist principally in an attempt to identify the Grendel story with Saxo's version of the corresponding story told about Bjarki.]

[Footnote 127: I, pp. 175-78.]

[Footnote 128: "Det ldste vidnesbyrd om sagnet bar vi i den skaldte *V[o.]lusp in skamma*; det hedder her: 'eru v[o.]lur allar fr Violfi.' Denne troldkvindernes stamfader er identisk med troldmanden Vit[h]olphus i Sakses norske saga; og nr vi ser, hvorledes digtets troldmandsremser nvner kendte sagnfigurer—Heir i *Volusp*; Hrossjfr i Sakses norske Baldersagn—, tr vi ogs i Violfr se hentydning til en bestemt digtning, *i.e.*, til dette norske Skjoldungsagn. Desvrre kendes digtets alder ikke videre nje; det er efterhedensk og er digtet som et tillg til *Volusp*, sikkert efter at dette digt var blevet udvidet med dvrgremserne. (F. Jnsson, *Oldn. lit. hist.*, I, 204, gr det til islandsk og stter det til 2. halvdel af 12te rh.)."—Olrik's note.]

[Footnote 129: See pp. 9, 15, 24.]

[Footnote 130: *St. Sag. Eng.*, pp. 120-21.]

[Footnote 131: See R. Imelmann's edition, pp. 45 ff.]

[Footnote 132: "*Hroarr-Helgi.* Frodas, der Florencius gegenbersteht und Waldeus zu beseitigen sucht, hat zwar als Usurpator in einem ganzen Typus seine Verwandten, aber eine in formeller Hinsicht auffallende in der nordischen Sage von Hroarr und Helgi. Hier stellt Froi zwei Neffen nach, die aber durch ihren Erzieher in Sicherheit gebracht werden. Sie rchen sich spter an dem Usurpator in seiner Halle. Bei seinen Nachstellungen lsst Froi sich tuschen. Fr diese Zge bietet der Waldeus eine genaue parallele (S. 45-60). Seine Vorlage konnte die Sage kennen, da sie in England entstanden und beliebt war; und ihre Benutzung mSste angenommen werden, sobald man die Namensgleichheit Froi—Froda (Frode) fr nicht zuflig hlt. Der Name Froi scheint in England sonst zu fehlen; er steht nicht bei Bjrkman."—-*Hist. Reg. Wald.*, Introd., p. 52.]

[Footnote 133: *St. Sag. Eng.*, pp. 103 ff.]

[Footnote 134: *St. Sag. Eng.*, p. 134.]

[Footnote 135: *Hist. Mer.*, Introd., p. 30.]

[Footnote 136: *St. Sag. Eng.*, p. 139.]

[Footnote 137: See, for instance, *Dan. Nor. Rig.*]

[Footnote 138: *Hist. Mer.*, Introd., pp. 65-67.]

[Footnote 139: The version of the Havelok story here referred to is that contained in Geffrei Gaimar's *Estorie des Engles* and summarized in *St. Sag. Eng.*, pp. 98-100.]

[Footnote 140: *Hist. Mer.*, Introd., p. 30, n.]

[Footnote 141: See *Helt.*, I, pp. 22-23.]

[Footnote 142: *Hist. Mer.*, p. 8.]

[Footnote 143: *Hist. Mer.*, p. 9.]

[Footnote 144: *Hist. Mer.*, p. 8.]

[Footnote 145: *Hist. Mer.*, p. 9.]

[Footnote 146: *Gest. Dan.*, p. 218.]

[Footnote 147: *St. Sag. Eng.*, p. 129.]

[Footnote 148: *Hist. Mer.*, Introd., p. 31.]

[Footnote 149: See pp. 86 ff.]

[Footnote 150: A variant of "Svil" in the manuscripts is "Svar." See *Hrs. Bjark.*, pp. 3, n. and 5, n.]

[Footnote 151: *Chron.*, V, p. 269.]

[Footnote 152: *Chron.*, V, p. 269.]

[Footnote 153: There is something similar to this in *Meriadoc*. Orwen, the princess, marries the King of Scotland. This feature of *Meriadoc*, besides being in line with Hroar's marrying Northri's daughter, points toward Scotland also.]

[Footnote 154: Siward married lfld, daughter of Ealdred, Earl of Bernicia in Northumbria (see p. 13).]

[Footnote 155: *Nor. Hist.*, I, pp. 180-81.]

[Footnote 156: *Macb.*, Introd., p. 15.]

[Footnote 157: *Chron.*, V, p. 274.]

[Footnote 168: Quoted by Langebek in *Sc. Rer. Dan.*, III. p. 291, n.]

[Footnote 159: Olrik; see p. 65.]

[Footnote 160: *Skjs.* (*Aarb.*, pp. 110 ff.).]

[Footnote 161: *Oldn. Lit. Hist.*, II, p. 665.]

[Footnote 162: See pp. 64 ff., where Olrik's explanation of the development in the relations between Frothi and Halfdan, from the earliest to the latest account, is given in full.]

[Footnote 163: See p. 69.]

[Footnote 164: "Vi finder *Skjoldungasagas* kongerkke bekrftet i de andre skrifter. *Langfegatal* stemmer helt igennem i kongersekken og—p et enkelt punkt nr—ogs i slgstskabs-forholdene. Rolv krakes saga stemmer ligeledes; kun gr den sin konge Frode til Halvdans broder, ikke til hans brodersn som de to andre kilder. *Hervararsaga* bar forvansket nogle af de mindre vigtige konge-og dronningnavne, men har i det hele samme bygning af Skjoldungslgten. De p Island bevarede oldkvad (*Grottesangen*, *Bjarkeml*, *Brvallakvadet* og *Hyndlulj*) stemmer belt med prosaskrifterne."—Olrik, *Aarb.*, p. 157.]

[Footnote 165: Son and successor of Scioldus.]

[Footnote 166: Said to have been king when Christ was born.]

[Footnote 167: Brothers, sons of Leifus.]

[Footnote 168: Married to Olafa, daughter of Vermundus.]

[Footnote 169: Chosen king upon the death of Frotho III, when Fridleus II was absent from the kingdom.]

[Footnote 170: Son and successor of Frotho III. He defeated Hiarnus and later slew him.]

[Footnote 171: Olaf appears here in a disturbing manner; but that Saxo had no clear conception of him is plain from the way he introduces his seventh book. He says: "Ingello quatuor filios fuisse, ex iisdemque, tribus bello consumptis, Olauum solum post patrem regnasse, perita rerum prodit antiquitas: quem quidam Ingelli sorore editum incerto opinionis arbitrio perhibent. Huius actus uetustatis squalore conspersos parum iusta noticia posteritatis apprehendit; extremum duntaxat prudencie eius monitum memoria uendicauit. Quippe cum supremis fati uiribus arctaretur, Frothoni et Haraldo filiis consulturus, alterum terris, alterum aquis regia dicione preesse, eamque potestatis differenciam non diutina usurpacione, sed annua uicissitudine sortini iubet."—*Gest. Dan.*, p. 216.]

[Footnote 172: Son of Ingjald, but not his successor on the throne.]

[Footnote 173: Halfdan in *Hrs.* and *Skjs.*]

[Footnote 174: Hroar in *Hrs.* and *Skjs.*]

[Footnote 175: Helgi in *Hrs.* and *Skjs.*]

[Footnote 176: *Beow.*, ll. 2024-69.]

[Footnote 177: *Beow.*, ll. 82-85.]

[Footnote 178: "Dette forhold, at det egenlige vikingeliv ligger forud for digtet, frer os hen til 10de rh. som dets tilblivelsestid."—*Helt.*, II, p. 36.]

[Footnote 179: *Helt.*, II, pp. 37-41. Olrik's notes, of which there are a number, have been omitted.]

[Footnote 180: Later, the statement is made that Hroar had a son called Waldar; but the statement causes no difficulty in this connection. First, we observe that when Hroar, who is older than Helgi, is slain, Helgi's son, Hrolf Kraki, becomes sole King of Denmark with no competitor for the throne. Secondly, Arngrim says: "Roas. Hujus posteros etsi non repperi in compendio unde Regum Dani Fragmenta descripsi; tamen genealogiam hanc alibi sic oblatam integre ut sequitur visum est contexere. Valderus cogn. munificus, Ro prdicti filius."—*Aarb.*, p. 139, n.]

[Footnote 181: Halfdan's brother, who, after Halfdan's death, married his widow, Sigrith.]

[Footnote 182: This is not expressly stated; but her appearance and action in the last scene admit of no other conclusion. This is Finnur Jnsson's opinion also; see p. 95, n.]

[Footnote 183: *Helt.*, I, pp. 173-74.]

[Footnote 184: Finnur Jnsson, in his comment on the *Frattr*, regards the version of the Hroar-Helgi story contained in the *Skj[o.]ldungasaga* and the *Bjarkarmur* as earlier than the version contained in the *Hrlfssaga*. His most significant statements bearing on the matter are as follows: "I *Skj[o.]ldungasaga*, der blandt de islandske kilder har strst betydning, har vi herfor [i.e., instead of Halfdan and Frothi] Hlfdan og Ingjaldr, der er halvbrdre, bgge snner af kong Fri froekni; Halvdans moder er en datter af kong Jrund i Sverrig, Ingjalds moder er en datter af Sverting og Frodes virkelige hustru; herom ved vor saga alts intet. Halvdan er ifg. *Skj.* gift med en Sigrr (sledes ogs i *Hrs.*, hvor hun pludselig dukker op). Deres brn er de samme som i sagaen; ogs her er Sign gift med Svil. Ingjald drber sin broder Halvdan og gifter sig med hans enke (heri finder vi motivet til at hun lader sig indebrnde med Frode i *Hrs.*, hvilket dr str ganske umotiveret)."—*Hrs. Bjark.*, Introd., p. 9.

The *Skj[o.]ldungasaga* does not, however, say that Ingjald's mother was a daughter of Swerting. It says, "Postea ducta alia, Ingialldum filium legitimum hredem suscepit" (*Aarb.*, p. 111). And later it says that Ingjald married Swerting's daughter. The words of the saga are, "Ingialldus Frodonis filius Svertingi baronis paulo ante commemorati filiam in uxorem accepit firmioris grati, ut omnibus visum, conciliand ergo" (*Aarb.*, p. 112). This would indicate that Ingjald was not the son of a daughter of Swerting.]

[Footnote 185: "Arngrim tilfjer, at natten efter var de hos en bonde, *i.e.*, Hrane, hvis gaver de afslog. (Footnote. Her trffer vi sikkert det oprindelige forhold, kun t mode med Odin.) Hvorledes Rolv rejste videre, siges ikke i nogen af kilderne. Det er klart heraf, at Arngrims fremstilling str sagaen nrmere end *Skj.*, hvilket nppe kommer af, at Snorre skulde have udeladt det som Arngrim har; det har vret den yngre bearbejdelse af *Skj.*, som A. Olrik vistnok med rette har ment at kunne pvise, som Arngrims fremstilling beror p."—Finnur Jnsson, *Hrs. Bjark.*, Introd., p. 25.]

[Footnote 186: See, for instance, Sarrazin's *Knig Hrodhgeirr und seine familie*; *Eng. Stud.*, XXIII, pp. 221 ff.]

[Footnote 187: *Aarb.*, pp. 164.]

[Footnote 188: See p. 85.]

[Footnote 189: *Beow.-Stud.*, pp. 41 ff., and *Eng. Stud.*, XXIII, p. 228.]

[Footnote 190: *Notes, Beow.*, pp. 43.]